GEOLOGY OF DEVILS TOWER NATIONAL MONUMENT

Prepared for

DEVILS TOWER NATURAL HISTORY ASSOCIATION

by

Charles S. Robinson and Robert E. Davis

Copyright, 1995, Mineral Systems, Inc.

FRONTISPIECE

Devils Tower from northeast

CONTENTS

Page

ABSTRACT 1

INTRODUCTION 3
HISTORY OF GEOLOGIC STUDIES
      DEVILS TOWER 5

GEOLOGY 7
    <u>Stratigraphy</u> 9
        Spearfish Formation 11
        Gypsum Spring Formation 13
        Sundance Formation 14
        Stockade Beaver Shale Member. 14
        Hulett Sandstone Member. 15
        Lak Member 17
        Redwater Shale Member. 17
        Morrison Formation 22
    <u>Igneous Rocks</u> 23
        Devils Tower Phonolite Porphyry 23
        Intrusive Breccia 26
        Age 30
    <u>Surficial Deposits</u> 31
        Stream Terrace Deposits and Alluvium 31
        Talus and Landslides 34
    <u>Structure</u> 44
        Sedimentary Rocks 44
        Igneous Rock 45

GEOLOGIC HISTORY 53

ORIGIN OF DEVILS TOWER 57

SUMMARY AND CONCLUSIONS 84

ACKNOWLEDGMENTS 87

REFERENCES 88

APPENDIX A 91
    Chart of Geologic Time 91

GLOSSARY 92

ILLUSTRATIONS

    Page

Frontispiece
    Devils Tower from northeast .... Preface
Figure 1: Map showing location of Devils Tower National Monument,
    Crook County, Wyoming 4
Figure 2 - Geologic Map, Devils Tower National Monument Area, Wyoming 8
Figure 3 - Generalized stratigraphic column of the sedimentary rocks of the Devils
    Tower Area, Wyoming 10
Figure 4 - Valley wall below east side of Devils Tower showing sedimentary rocks 12
Figure 5. Lak Member above Hulett Sandstone Member, Sundance Formation,
    northeast of Devils Tower 16
Figure 6. Fossil Hill (center foreground) and area underlain by Redwater Shale
    Member, Sundance Formation, northwest of Devils Tower 18
Figure 7. Outcrops of fossiliferous limestone, Fossil Hill, northwest of Devils Tower. 20
Figure 8. Sample from Fossil Hill showing Ostrea sp, Devils Tower National Monument 21
Figure 9. Photograph of rock from Devils Tower showing rock texture 24
Figure 10. Photograph of granitic clast from Intrusive Breccia. 27
Figure 11. Photograph of Devils Tower and Missouri Buttes. (Distance about 4 miles) ...29
Figure 12. Prairie dog town east of Devils Tower. Town is on an alluvial terrace 33
Figure 13. Photograph of Devils Tower showing talus apron around the base of
    Devils Tower (U.S. National Park Service photograph) 35
Figure 14. Youngest talus at base of Devils Tower, west side 37
Figure 15. Photograph of snow on Devils Tower, southwest side. 38
Figure 16. Talus of intermediate age, west side of Devils Tower. 39
Figure 17. Talus next to oldest in age, west side of Devils Tower 40
Figure 18. Talus blocks of Hulett Sandstone Member lying on Stockade Beaver Shale
    Member, Sundance Formation, south side of Devils Tower. 42
Figure 19. Talus blocks of sandstone and quartzite about 1,400 feet north of Devils Tower. .43
    A. Area of talus blocks 43
    B. Blocks of quartzite 43
Figure 20. West side of Devils Tower showing massive base, shoulder, main
    columnar section, and crest 47
Figure 21. Base and shoulder of Devils Tower, west side, showing irregular joints
    of base merging into almost horizontal joints of shoulder 48
Figure 22. Crest section of Devils Tower, northwest side, showing irregularly
    shaped and cross-jointed column 50
Figure 23. A talus block derived from the crest area of Devils Tower showing
    cross-joints. (Block about 20 feet long) 52
Figure 24. Generalized section of the sedimentary rocks of the western flanks of the
    Black Hills, Wyoming 54
Figure 25. Map showing location of Mount Taylor volcanic field, New Mexico 60
Figure 26. Schematic diagram showing the origin of the volcanic necks of the
    Mt. Taylor region, New Mexico. A, prior to erosion, B, after erosion 63

Figure 27. Cabezon Peak, showing outcrops of sandstone at base, talus apron,
and columnar joints, Mt. Taylor volcanic field, New Mexico 65
Figure 28. Columnar joints, Cabezon Peak, Mt. Taylor volcanic field, New Mexico 66
Figure 29. Cerro de Nuestra Señora, from the west, showing sedimentary rock
below base. Mt. Taylor volcanic field, New Mexico 68
Figure 30. Map showing locations of intrusive rocks, western Black Hills, Wyoming 72
Figure 31. Geologic Cross-section through Devils Tower, Wyoming,
at time of emplacement 80
Figure 32. Geologic Cross-section through Devils Tower, Wyoming, at present time 81
Figure 33. Devils Tower at Sunset, west face 86

TABLES

Page

Table 1 - Modal analyses[1] of Devils Tower phonolite porphyry
(From Halvorson, 1980, Table 2, p. 40) 25
Table 2 - Ages of intrusive igneous rocks, western flank Black Hills, Wyoming 76

GEOLOGY OF DEVILS TOWER, WYOMING

Charles S. Robinson and Robert E. Davis

Abstract

Devils Tower is the most conspicuous physiographic feature on the western flank of the Black Hills of Wyoming. Because of its striking appearance, it was established in 1906 as the first National Monument. Its most prominent feature is the columnar jointing, which has been used by most geologists to interpret the origin of the Tower.

Devils Tower is composed of phonolite porphyry, a hard crystalline rock, and is one of a series of igneous intrusions of similar composition that intruded the sedimentary rocks of the western flank of the Black Hills 55 Ma to 33 Ma (before the present). The sedimentary rocks, which overlie Precambrian igneous and metamorphic rocks, range in age from Cambrian to Oligocene. Exposed at the base of Devils Tower is the Sundance Formation of Jurassic age and, in the vicinity of the Tower, are the Gypsum Spring Formation of Middle Jurassic age, and the Spearfish Formation of Triassic age. The Morrison Formation, of Jurassic age, is exposed northwest of the Tower.

The origin of Devils Tower has been attributed to 1) an igneous intrusion, or plug, that intruded the sedimentary rocks but did not reach the surface, 2) to the remnant of a laccolith, and 3) to the neck of an extinct volcano. The volcanic-neck origin is based primarily on a similarity of the columnar jointing of the Tower to the columnar jointing in volcanic necks exposed in the Mount Taylor volcanic field of New Mexico. The columnar jointing is the only similarity between the volcanic necks and Devils Tower. The volcanic necks are composed of basalt breccia, or andesite, showing considerable variation in mineralogy, texture, and structure within the same neck. They were vents for magma that repeatedly poured out to form many square miles of primarily basalt flows. In contrast, Devils Tower consists of phonolite porphyry, an intermediate to silicic rock, which, in general, is homogeneous in mineralogy, texture, and structure. There is no evidence of extrusive igneous rock in the vicinity of Devils Tower, and at the time of the intrusion of Devils Tower (50 ∞ Ma), the total stratigraphic section above the present level of the top of Devils Tower was approximately 7,000 feet. The White River Formation, younger than Devils Tower, does not include pyroclastic material.

On the basis of the regional and local geology, and the mineralogy, texture, and structure of Devils Tower, it is concluded that Devils Tower is the remnant of an igneous intrusion that did not breach the surface. The intrusive magma reached the level of the Lower Cretaceous shale where it expanded to an inverted teardrop shape. The columnar joints formed as the magma cooled. The present Tower shape is the result of removal by erosion of the intruded, relatively soft sedimentary rocks and the weathering and erosion of the relatively hard columnar jointed igneous rock of the Tower.

INTRODUCTION

Devils Tower, a mass of bare rock, which rises abruptly from the surrounding grassland and pine forests, is one of the most conspicuous features on the west flank of the Black Hills of Wyoming (Frontispiece). Because of its striking appearance it was used as the background for the movie "Close Encounters of the Third Kind," produced and directed by Steven Spielberg for Columbia Pictures.

Devils Tower National Monument includes an area of about $2^{1/2}$ square miles near the center of Crook County, Wyoming (Fig. 1). Because of the scenic beauty and scientific interest, President Theodore Roosevelt in 1906 established Devils Tower and a small surrounding area as the first National Monument. A paved road, State Highway 24, extends about 7 miles south from the Monument and joins U.S. Highway 14, which in turn joins U.S. Interstate Highway 90 at Moorecroft, about 33 miles to the southwest, and at Sundance, about 29 miles to the southeast. The entrance to the Monument may be reached also by State Highway 24 that extends northeastward via Hulett and Aladdin, Wyoming to Belle Fourche, South Dakota — a distance of about 54 miles — where it joins U.S. Highways 85 and 212.

The senior author (Robinson, 1956) first prepared a report on the geology of Devils Tower National Monument in 1956 in support of the 50th anniversary celebration of the First National Monument, while he was employed by the U.S. Geological Survey in a regional study of the northern and western flanks of the Black Hills (Robinson, Mapel, and Bergendahl, 1964). The associate author, Robert E. Davis, also was working for the U.S. Geological Survey on the west side of the Black Hills at this time (Bergendahl, Davis, and Izett, 1961; Davis and Izett, 1962). From 1993 to 1995, with the encouragement of the National Park Service, they agreed to revise the original U.S. Geological Survey

Bulletin 1021-I and prepare a new topographic and geologic map of Devils Tower National Monument. This report represents the latest documentation on the geology of Devils Tower National Monument. The topographic and geologic maps are published separately.

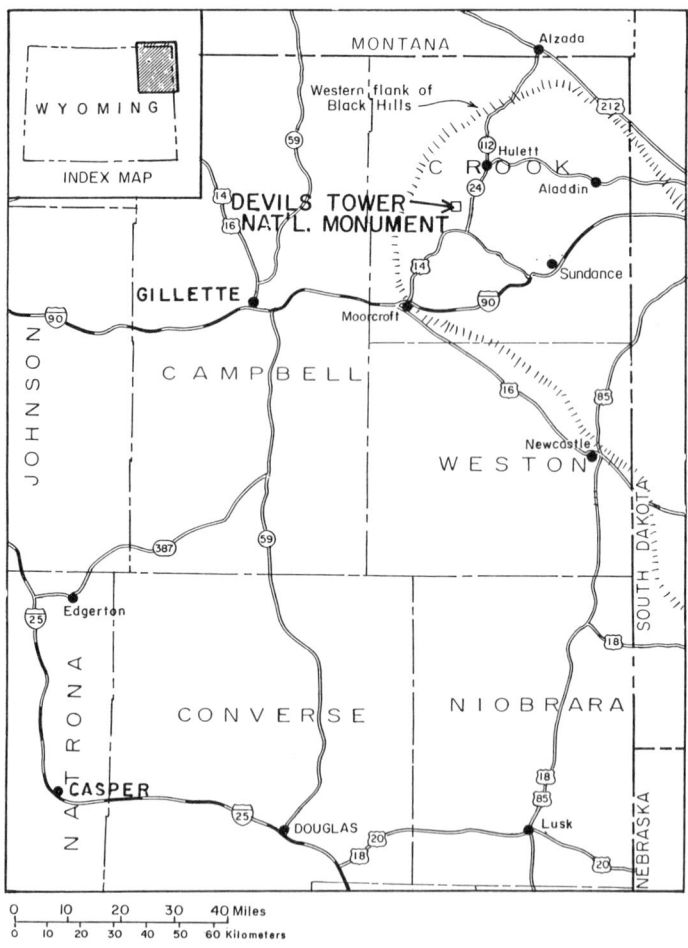

FIGURE 1:

Map showing location of Devils Tower National Monument, Crook County, Wyoming

HISTORY OF GEOLOGIC STUDIES DEVILS TOWER

Native Americans worshipped at Devils Tower long before the appearance of the white man. Their legends attributed the columns on the side of the Tower to a giant bear scratching on the sides of the sacred butte to try to reach seven little girls, who in trying to escape from the bear, jumped on a low rock and prayed to the rock to save them. The rock heard them and grew so high that the bear couldn't reach them (Mattison, 1967, p. 3). Early fur trappers undoubtedly saw the Tower, but the first description of the Tower was the result of the early geographic and geologic surveys of the west by the U.S. Government.

A report prepared by Newton and Jenney (1880) on the Geology and Resources of the Black Hills of Dakota, as part of the Government's Geographic and Geologic Survey of the Rocky Mountain Region, was the first time the geology of Devils Tower was noted. Newton and Jenney viewed the Tower, and Missouri Buttes (also called Little Missouri Buttes), in 1875 from the summit of Warren Peak in the Bear Lodge Mountains, and then visited both. They referred to Devils Tower as Bear Lodge Butte (Mato Tipila Paha) and gave a brief description of the Tower and its composition and structure. Carpenter (1888), in notes on the geology of the Black Hills, referred to Devils Tower as Bear Butte. Pirsson (1894) described the rock of Devils Tower and Missouri Buttes. Russell (1896) in his study of the "Igneous Intrusion in the Neighborhood of the Black Hills" gave a description of the Tower and the rocks around its base. He referred to it as Bear Butte or Mato Teepee. Jagger (1901), in a study of the laccoliths of the Black Hills, described Devils Tower and Missouri Buttes.

The first geologic mapping of the area of Devils Tower was done by Darton and O'Hara (1907). Darton (1909), in his study of geology and water resources of the northern Black Hills, gave an additional description of Devils Tower and its origin. Effinger

(1934), on behalf of the National Park Service, summarized the geology of Devils Tower National Monument primarily on the basis of the work done by Darton and O'Hara (1907). A special study of just the jointing in Devils Tower was made by Dutton and Swartz (1936).

The senior author, while making a regional study of the geology of the western flanks of the Black Hills (Robinson, Mapel, and Bergendahl, 1964), prepared a report on the geology of Devils Tower National Monument for the 50th Anniversary of the first National Monument (Robinson, 1956), and later presented a paper on the origin of Devils Tower (Robinson, 1960).

Except for isotopic age dating of the rock (McDowell, 1971; Hill, Izett, and Naeser, 1975) no further studies were made of the geology of the Devils Tower area, until the work of Halvorson (1980). As partial fulfillment of the requirements of a Doctor of Philosophy Degree at the University of North Dakota, Halvorson conducted an excellent study of the geology, particularly the petrography and petrology, of Devils Tower, Missouri Buttes, and the Barlow Canyon area.

GEOLOGY

The geology of Devils Tower National Monument is relatively simple. On approaching the Tower, one sees a striking fluted column of igneous rock standing on a platform of brightly-colored sedimentary rock layers that form the limits of the valley of the Belle Fourche River (Frontispiece). Surrounding the base of the Tower is an apron of talus, which is composed of blocks of rock derived from the Tower, and much of the highlands in the area are covered by colluvium, or soil, derived from the weathering of the bedrock. Along the Belle Fourche River are terraces of alluvium and alluvium deposited by the river. (Fig. 2).

Igneous rocks are rocks that have cooled from molten material such as lava. Sedimentary rocks are composed of grains of material that have been deposited by wind or water on land or in water.

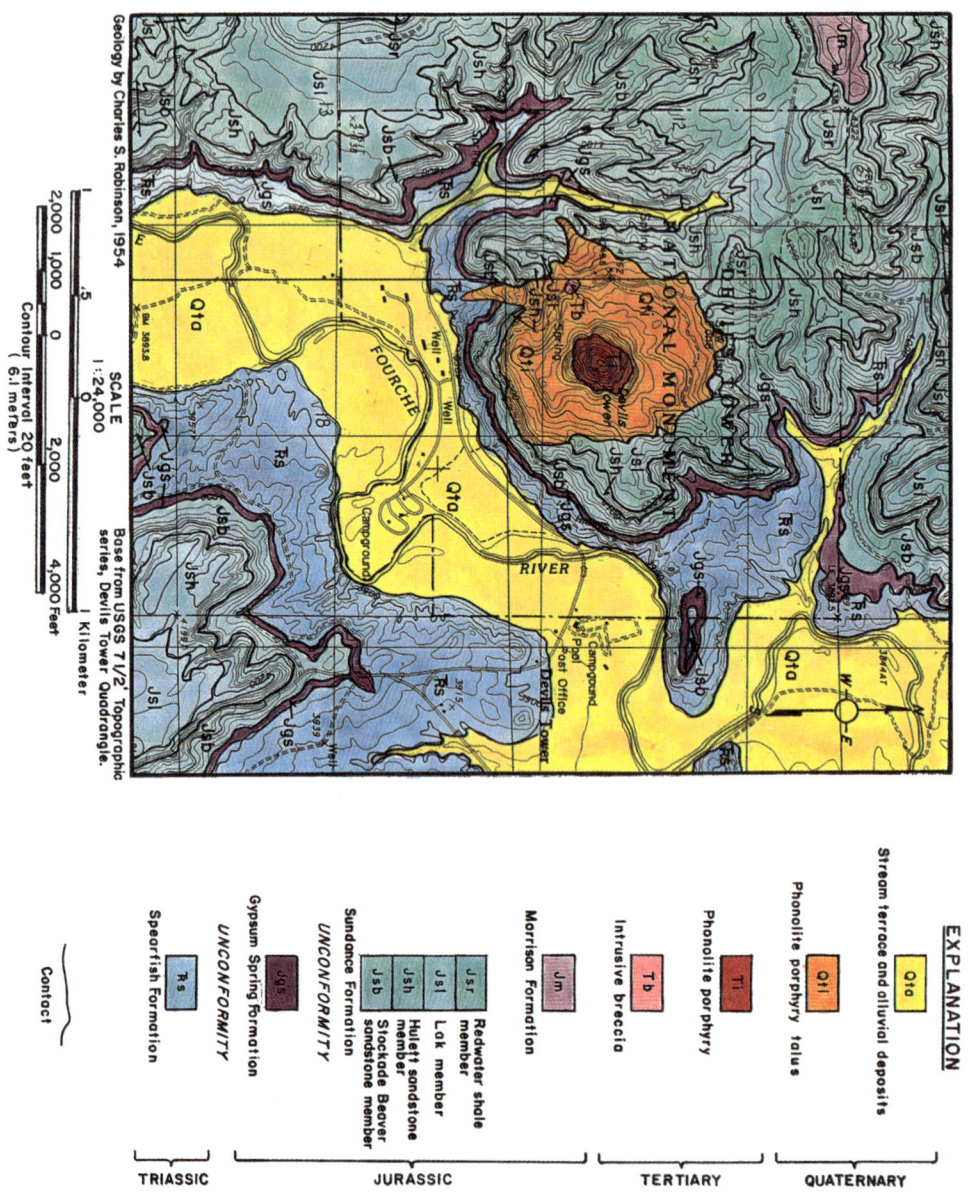

FIGURE 2:

Geologic Map, Devils Tower National Monument Area, Wyoming

STRATIGRAPHY

The sedimentary rocks exposed in the Devils Tower area are shown in a generalized column on Figure 3. This figure shows the geologic age, formation and member name, the range in thickness, and the lithology, and gives a brief description of each sedimentary rock unit. The rocks range in age from Triassic to Upper Jurassic (Appendix A). They are divided, from oldest to youngest, into the Spearfish Formation; the Gypsum Spring Formation; the Sundance Formation, which includes the Stockade Beaver Shale Member, the Hulett Sandstone Member, the Lak Member, and the Redwater Shale Member; and the Morrison Formation. The sedimentary rocks that surround Devils Tower have a total exposed thickness of about 400 ft.

Stratigraphy: the science of rock strata, concerned with sequence, age, composition, fossil content, and distribution of sedimentary rocks.

Geologists have divided the rocks in the crust of the earth into different ages that are determined by major geologic events, such as periods of mountain building. See Appendix A.

Geologists divide sedimentary rocks into formations, and some formations into members, on the basis of differences in composition and age. The formations and members are named for the areas in which they are best exposed, i.e., the Sundance Formation is named for Sundance, Wyoming, and the Hulett Sandstone Member is named for Hulett, Wyoming, just north of Devils Tower.

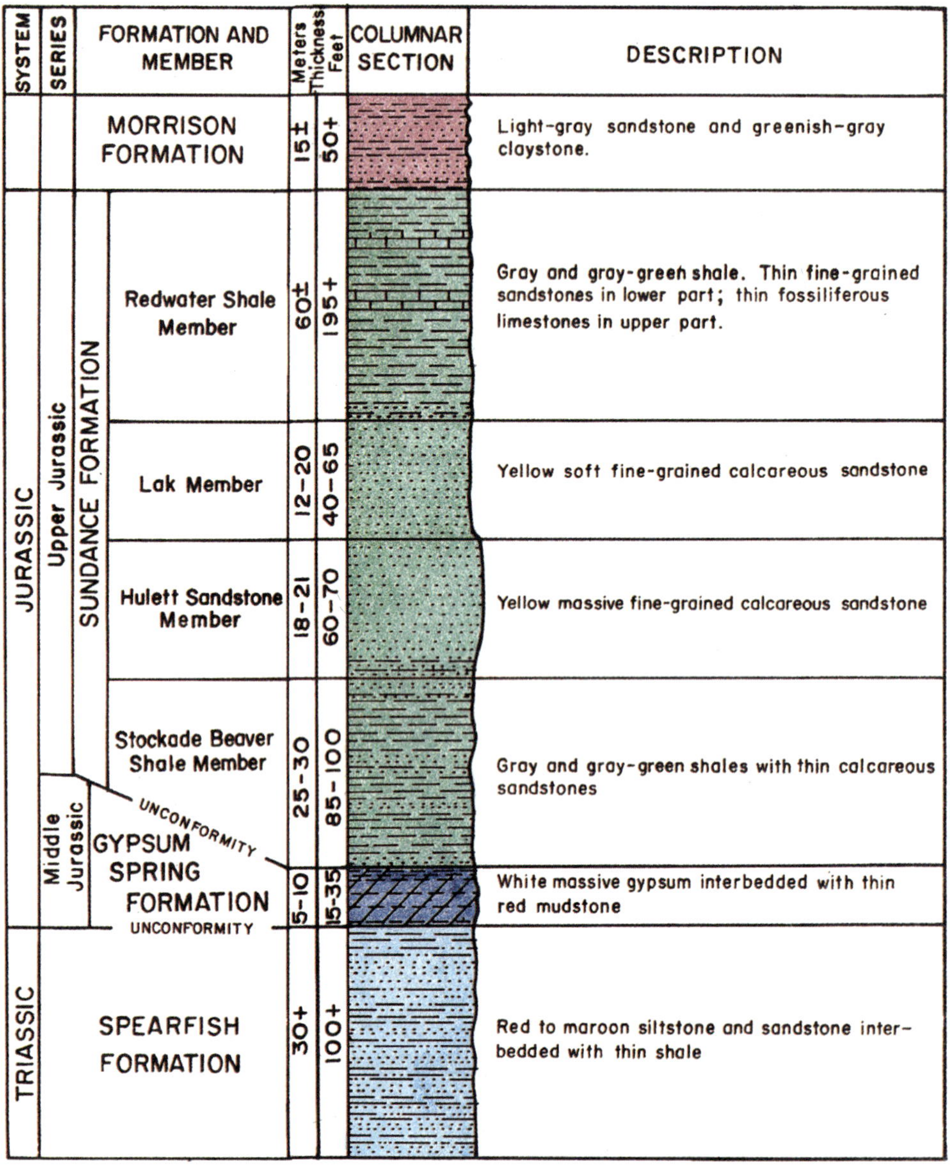

SYSTEM	SERIES	FORMATION AND MEMBER	Meters Thickness	Feet	COLUMNAR SECTION	DESCRIPTION
JURASSIC	Upper Jurassic	MORRISON FORMATION	15±	50+		Light-gray sandstone and greenish-gray claystone.
		SUNDANCE FORMATION — Redwater Shale Member	60±	195+		Gray and gray-green shale. Thin fine-grained sandstones in lower part; thin fossiliferous limestones in upper part.
		Lak Member	12–20	40–65		Yellow soft fine-grained calcareous sandstone
		Hulett Sandstone Member	18–21	60–70		Yellow massive fine-grained calcareous sandstone
		Stockade Beaver Shale Member	25–30	85–100		Gray and gray-green shales with thin calcareous sandstones
	Middle Jurassic	GYPSUM SPRING FORMATION (UNCONFORMITY)	5–10	15–35		White massive gypsum interbedded with thin red mudstone
TRIASSIC		SPEARFISH FORMATION	30+	100+		Red to maroon siltstone and sandstone interbedded with thin shale

FIGURE 3:

Generalized stratigraphic column of the sedimentary rocks of the Devils Tower Area, Wyoming

Spearfish Formation

The Spearfish Formation crops out in the southern and northeastern parts of Devils Tower National Monument along the valley of the Belle Fourche River and its tributaries, and forms conspicuous brownish-red to maroon cliffs that border the Belle Fourche River valley for several miles in the Devils Tower region. The formation is 450 to 825 feet thick in the northern Black Hills area (Robinson, Mapel, and Bergendahl, 1964, p. 9), however, only the uppermost 100 feet are exposed within the National Monument.

The Spearfish Formation consists of red to maroon siltstone and sandstone interbedded with mudstone or shale. Locally, greenish-blue shale partings are found in the siltstone and sandstone. The formation is poorly cemented and weathers very easily to form, for the most part, gentle slopes, as on the northeast and southwest sides of the monument. Where it does form cliffs, such as south of the Tower, the cliffs are cut by many sharp gullies (Fig. 4).

No fossils have been found in the Spearfish Formation in the Devils Tower region, but elsewhere in Wyoming, stratigraphically equivalent rocks contain land vertebrates of Triassic age.

Siltstone, rock composed of silt grains.

Sandstone, rock composed of sand grains.

Shale, rock composed of clay that breaks into thin pieces.

FIGURE 4:

Valley wall below east side of Devils Tower showing sedimentary rocks

GYPSUM SPRING FORMATION

The Gypsum Spring Formation is exposed in a thin but almost continuous band around the Tower on the southwest to northeast sides. It also crops out near the top of the small hill at the east boundary of the Monument, a few hundred feet north of the Entrance Station. This formation is composed mostly of white gypsum, which stands out conspicuously between the red beds of the underlying Spearfish Formation and beds of gray-green shale at the base of the overlying Sundance Formation (Fig. 4).

The Gypsum Spring Formation ranges in thickness from about 15 to about 35 feet. It is thickest on the hill at the east boundary of the Monument where it is made up of a lower unit consisting of a bed of white massive gypsum 20 feet thick overlain by 14 feet of interbedded white gypsum and dark-maroon mudstone. The formation is 15 feet thick along the cliff directly south of Devils Tower. At this location, the formation consists of 12 feet of white massive gypsum with interbedded 1 to 6-inch thick beds of dark-maroon mudstone overlain by 3 feet of dark-brownish-red mudstone. The differences in thicknesses are primarily the result of erosion of the Gypsum Spring Formation prior to the deposition of the Stockade Beaver Shale Member of the Sundance Formation (Imlay, 1947, p. 243)

No fossils have been found in the Gypsum Spring Formation in the Devils Tower area. Ostracodes, of the genus *Cytherella*, were found northeast of the Tower in the SW 1/4 sec 13. T. 55 N., R. 64 W. (Robinson, et al, 1964, p. 11).

Gypsum: a white mineral composed of calcium sulfate.

Ostracodes: a microscopic shelled animal.

SUNDANCE FORMATION

The Sundance Formation consists of an alternating sequence of greenish-gray shale, light-gray to yellowish-brown sandstone and siltstone, and gray limestone. The formation crops out above the gypsum and red shale of the Gypsum Spring Formation on the bluffs and low rolling hills that surround the Tower. The formation consists of four members that are, in order of age from oldest to youngest, the Stockade Beaver Shale Member, the Hulett Sandstone Member, the Lak Member, and the Redwater Shale Member (Fig. 3) (Imlay, 1947, p. 227-273.)

Stockade Beaver Shale Member. — In general, this member, because it is composed mostly of shale, is poorly exposed. The best exposures of the lower part of this member are on the hill at the east boundary of the Monument (Fig. 4) and along the steep slope south of the Tower. The upper part of this member is fairly well exposed on the south side of the ridge north of the Tower. The member has a thickness of 85 to 100 feet.

The composition differs considerably in detail from one exposure to another, but in general it consists of gray-green shale with interbedded fine-grained calcareous sandstone. At the base of the member, at nearly all exposures, is a thin sandstone, 1 to 24 inches thick, containing black or dark-gray water-worn chert pebbles that have a maximum dimension of about 2 inches. Above this basal sandstone, the lower half of the member is composed mostly of gray-green shale, which locally contains some interbedded fine-grained calcareous sandstone, thin sandy and shaly limestone or dolomitic limestone, and rarely thin beds of red mudstone. The upper half of the member consists of dark-gray to

Limestone: rock composed of calcium carbonate.

Calcareous: lime cement or grains coated with lime, calcium carbonate.

Chert: a rock composed of amorphous, or uncrystallized, silica oxide.

gray-green shale with interbedded fine-grained calcareous sandstone beds that range from less than 1 foot to 6 feet in thickness.

The contact of the Stockade Beaver Shale Member with the overlying Hulett Sandstone Member is gradational. The sandstone becomes more abundant in the upper part of the Stockade Beaver Shale, and the contact between those two members is placed at that point where the sandstone makes up more than 50 percent of the rocks.

Hulett Sandstone Member. — The Hulett Sandstone Member is resistant to weathering and forms conspicuous, almost vertical cliffs that nearly encircle the Tower. This member ranges in thickness from about 60 to 70 feet.

The Hulett Sandstone Member consists, in general, of massive fine-grained glauconitic calcareous sandstone. It is typically yellow or brownish yellow but locally may be pink or red. In the lower 5 to 10 feet the sandstone is in beds from less than 1 inch to 2 feet thick separated by gray or greenish-gray shale partings of from less than 1 inch to 6 inches thick. Many of the sandstone beds at the base of the member are ripple marked.

The 50 to 60 feet in the middle of the member consists of massive beds that range in thickness from 5 to 20 feet. This portion is well cemented and forms the conspicuous cliff seen throughout the area. The upper 5 to 10 feet is thin bedded (beds from less

---

Dolomitic: contains dolomite, which is a magnesium and calcium carbonate compared to limestone, which is only calcium carbonate.

Mudstone: rock composed of silt and clay.

Glauconitic: contains glauconite, a dull-green earthy or granular mineral of the mica group.

Ripple marks: formed on sand dunes, beaches or under shallow water by wind, waves, or currents.

FIGURE 5:
Lak Member above Hulett Sandstone Member, Sundance Formation, northeast of Devils Tower.

than 1 inch to 6 inches in thickness) locally shaly, and poorly cemented. This grades upward into the overlying sandstone and siltstone of the Lak Member.

Lak Member. — The Lak Member crops out above the cliff of Hulett Sandstone that almost encircles the Tower, and it underlies a broad rolling area in the northwestern part of the Monument. The member is rarely exposed because it is composed of soft sandstone and siltstone that usually weather to gentle slopes and become covered with vegetation. The best exposure is on the steep hill east of the Tower and northwest of the bridge across the Belle Fourche River (Fig. 5).

This member is 65 feet thick a few hundred feet east of the Tower, but mapping within the Monument and measured sections within a few miles of the Monument, indicate that the average thickness is about 45 feet.

The Lak Member is typically poorly bedded soft very fine grained calcareous sandstone and siltstone with a few thin gray-green sandy shale partings. At the base and near the top of the member may be a few thin (less than 1 inch to 6 inches thick) well-cemented sandstone beds that form small ridges. The sandstone and siltstone grade almost imperceptibly from one to the other. The color ranges from light yellow brown and yellow to red. In the Devils Tower area, shades of yellow and yellowish brown are most common.

The contact of the Lak Member with the overlying Redwater Shale Member can be observed only in the exposure east of the Tower. At this location, the upper 3 feet of the Lak Member is a yellowish-brown calcareous silty sandstone with a few discontinuous sandy shale partings (less than 1 inch thick), and the lower 3 feet of the overlying Redwater Shale Member consists of dark-gray-green shale with interbedded thin silty sandstone.

Redwater Shale Member. — This member encircles Devils Tower, but at most places it is covered by talus from the Tower.

FIGURE 6:

Fossil Hill (center foreground) and area underlain by Redwater Shale Member, Sundance Formation, northwest of Devils Tower.

Even where it is not covered by talus, it is poorly exposed. It consists mostly of shale that weathers into gentle slopes, which are usually covered by vegetation. The Redwater Shale Member is partly exposed on Fossil Hill, northwest of Devils Tower, and on the hill in the northwest corner of the Monument. The best exposures are on Fossil Hill (Fig. 6).

The top of the Redwater Shale Member is not exposed within the limits of the Monument; consequently, the thickness could not be determined. In surrounding areas, the Redwater Shale Member ranges in thickness from 150 to 190 feet. It is at least 100 feet thick on the hill in the northwest corner of the Monument.

The Redwater Shale Member consists mostly of light-gray to dark-gray-green soft shale. In the lower 20 or 30 feet are beds of soft yellow sandstone, 3 inches to 2 feet thick. In the upper part, ranging from 50 feet above the base to the top, are lenticular beds of fossiliferous limestone 1 inch to 4 feet thick. Two such beds of fossiliferous limestone are exposed on Fossil Hill (Fig. 7).

The Sundance Formation contains clams, oysters, belemnites (squids), and other marine fossils that establish its age as Late Jurassic. (Imlay, 1947, p. 244-264). No fossils were collected from the National Monument, but numerous collections were made from all around the Black Hills. Fossil Hill is composed mostly of *Ostrea* Sp, a small Jurassic-aged oyster (Fig. 8).

FIGURE 7:

Outcrops of fossiliferous limestone, Fossil Hill, northwest of Devils Tower.

FIGURE 8:

Sample from Fossil Hill showing *Ostrea* sp, Devils Tower National Monument.

Morrison Formation

The Morrison Formation does not occur within the boundaries of Devils Tower National Monument. It is exposed on the hill just west of the northwest corner of the Monument, and its location is shown on Figure 2.

The Morrison Formation is generally between 80 and 120 feet thick. Only the lower part, possibly 20 feet, is preserved northwest of the Monument, and is poorly exposed.

The basal bed of the Morrison Formation usually consists of light-gray sandstone or greenish-gray claystone or shale that rests conformably on a bed of yellow-weathering calcareous sandstone at the top of the Sundance Formation. Beds at the contact appear to represent a thin transitional zone from marine rocks below to nonmarine rocks above.

Discontinuous beds of limestone or marl, a few inches to as much as 4 feet thick, are interbedded with claystone in the lower calcareous part of the formation at all exposures, and limestone is also abundant in the claystone as small concretions or nodules as much as 4 inches in diameter. The limestone is light gray to grayish white and characteristically very finely crystalline to sublithographic. Some limestone beds are silty or sandy. Commonly, a ledge-forming bed of sandy limestone 1 to 2 feet thick with contorted gray laminae crops out within 10 feet stratigraphically of the base of the formation. (Robinson, Mapel, and Bergendahl, 1964, p. 19.)

Claystone: rock composed of clay that breaks into chunks.

Marl: soft earthy limestone.

Lithographic: very fine-grained limestone once used to make printing plates to produce lithographs.

IGNEOUS ROCKS

The igneous rocks in the area of Devils Tower make up the main mass of the Tower, and a small area of intrusive breccia.

DEVILS TOWER PHONOLITE PORPHYRY

The rock that comprises Devils Tower has been termed, based on petrographic studies, as trachyte (Newton and Jenney, 1880; Jagger, 1901), phonolite or phonolite porphyry (Pirsson, 1894; Johannson in Darton & O'Hara, 1907; Dutton and Schwartz, 1936; and Robinson, 1954), nepheline syenite (Robinson, Mapel, and Bergendahl, 1964), and analcime phonolite (Halvorson, 1980). The differences in terminology are primarily differences in terminology with time. In a fresh hand specimen, the rock is seen to consist of a light- to dark-gray or greenish-gray very fine grained groundmass with conspicuous crystals of white feldspar (anorthoclase) — commonly about 5 mm to 10 mm long — and smaller (1-5 mm) dark-green crystals of pyroxene (aegirine-augite) (Fig. 9). The following table, reproduced from Halvorson (1980, p. 40), the most recent and thorough petrographic study, gives the mineral composition of Devils Tower based on samples collected from all over the Tower.

Porphyry: an igneous rock that consists of large grains — phenocrysts — in a fine- grained ground mass.

Petrography or petrographic studies: is that branch of geology that deals with the description — mineral content and the relationship of minerals — and the systematic classification of rocks based on mineral composition and relationships.

Anorthoclase: a sodium-potassium-aluminum silicate of the alkali feldspar group.

Aegirine-augite: calcium-magnesium-iron aluminum silicate of the pyroxene group.

FIGURE 9.

Photograph of rock from Devils Tower showing rock texture.

Table 1 - Modal analyses[1] of Devils Tower phonolite porphyry
(From Halvorson, 1980, Table 2, p. 40)

Sample Number	T16	T31	T32	T26	T14	T122	T112	T101	T23	T115	T11	T12	T13
Phenocrysts[2]													
Anorthoclase[3]	31.2	23.4	24.4	37.2	36.0	17.5	29.3	33.6	32.4	21.6	34.9	26.9	28.5
Aegirine-augite	5.4	7.0	5.2	2.8	6.6	4.2	9.2	8.0	6.4	7.1	5.6	6.5	7.4
Sphene	0.6	0.2	1.2	x	x	0.8	0.4	x	0.4	x	x	x	0.3
Nepheline	0.5	x	x	x	x	x	x	x	x	x	x	x	x
Nosean	0.8	x	x	x	x	x	x	x	x	x	x	x	x
Groundmass and microphenocrysts	49.9	50.0	62.4	45.6	49.6	56.7	39.5	44.4	42.4	62.5	47.5	59.8	52.4
Albite and microcline	17.4	x	x	x	x	x	x	x	x	x	x	x	x
Analcime	19.7	x	x	x	x	x	x	x	x	x	x	x	x
Aegirine	12.8	x	x	x	x	x	x	x	x	x	x	x	x
Veins, pore-filling, and replacement													
Analcime	9.2	10.0	4.0	12.0	5.8	11.2	14.8	8.0	12.8	7.2	10.2	6.0	6.9
Calcite	2.2	0.6	x		0.6	3.2	0.8	0.4	4.0	0.4	1.0	x	4.3
Zeolite		4.4	x	0.8		1.6	0.4	2.4		0.6	0.6	0.8	x
Hematite	0.2	0.6	2.0		1.4		x	x	0.4	0.6	0.2		0.2
Clay		3.4	0.8	1.0		4.8	5.6	3.2	1.2				

x present but not point-counted.

1. Modal analyses are made by microscope and are the volume percent of the different minerals.
2. Phenocrysts are the mineral grains larger than those of the general groundmass.
3. Mineral compositions given in glossary.

INTRUSIVE BRECCIA

Along the trail about 500 feet south of the Visitors Center, and west of Devils Tower, is an area underlain by Intrusive Breccia. The breccia is completely surrounded by talus and the breccia is very poorly exposed. Only some of the large clasts that make up the breccia can be seen. Because of its distance from the Tower, and the fact that its relation to any other rock types cannot be determined because of the surrounding talus, there is some question if this exposure is in place. It is possible that a block of intrusive breccia, during the weathering of the Tower, broke free and moved downslope to its present position.

The intrusive breccia was termed agglomerate by Darton and O'Hara (1907, p. 6). They quoted Jagger (1901) as stating that the matrix appears to be composed of decomposed porphyry and the clasts included irregular fragments of granite, limestone, sandstone, quartzite, rhyolite, schist, shale, flint, and pegmatite ranging from less than 1 foot to more than 2 feet in diameter. Halvorson (1980, p. 58) termed this rock an "Alloclastic Breccia" but was not able, probably because of the extreme alteration, to do any petrographic studies of the matrix. Figure 10 is a photograph of a granitic clast from the intrusive breccia.

Breccia: rock composed of fragments of other older rocks.

Clasts: the larger fragments in a breccia or conglomerate.

Conglomerate: sedimentary rock composed of cobbles and gravel.

Rhyolite: composition similar to granite but very fine grained.

Schist: metamorphic rock, one changed by heat and pressure, that breaks into thin flat pieces.

Flint: amorphous silica oxide.

Pegmatite: coarse-grained granite.

FIGURE 10.

Photograph of granitic clast from Intrusive Breccia.

A similar intrusive breccia is associated with the Missouri Buttes, about 4 miles west of Devils Tower. This breccia is well exposed and was described by Robinson, Mapel, and Bergendahl (1964, p. 108) as consisting of: (Fig. 11)

> "rounded to subrounded fragments of sedimentary and igneous rocks, from less than 1 to 30 mm in diameter, and rounded to angular mineral grains, in a vesicular aphanitic groundmass. The fragments consist of gray limestone; greenish-gray argillite; yellowish- to reddish-brown siltstone; reddish-brown fine-grained sandstone; rounded quartz and chert pebbles and grains; angular grains of feldspar including orthoclase, microcline, sanidine, anorthoclase, and plagioclase; biotite granite; and a grayish-white aphanitic porphyry with phenocrysts of feldspar. The groundmass is so fine grained and altered that the constituent minerals could not be identified. At least half the groundmass is isotropic and is probably glass. Some of the vesicles are lined with zeolites and calcite, and possibly unidentified alteration products."

Argillite: compact rock derived from mudstone or shale by compaction.

Feldspars: sodium, potassium, calcium aluminum silicates.

Aphanitic: igneous rock so fine grained that the individual grains cannot be seen with the unaided eye.

Isotropic: a material that transmits light at the same speed in all directions; a glass.

FIGURE 11.

Photograph of Devils Tower and Missouri Buttes. (Distance about 4 miles)

AGE

The age of Devils Tower has been measured from the K-AR ratios on alkali feldspar and by the fission-track method on sphene. The analyses of the feldspar gave an age of 40.5∞ 1.6 Ma (Bassett, 1961, p. 1373). The fission-track method gave an age of 53.3∞ 6.8 Ma (Hill, Izett, and Naeser, 1975, p. 61). They noted that the alkali feldspar analyses give an age for Devils Tower younger than that determined by the fission-track method. They considered it probable that the younger age was the result of the loss of argon from unmixed alkali feldspar. This is also presumably the age of the intrusive breccia.

Zeolites: hydrous aluminum silicates analogous in composition to feldspars.

K-AR: The ratio of potassium to argon in the rock. Argon radioactively decays at a constant rate to give potassium. From the ratio, the age can be calculated.

Ma: Millions of years before the present; e.g., 55 Ma = 55 million years ago.

Fission Track Dating: a method of calculating an age in years by determining the ratio of the spontaneous fission-track density to induced fission tracks (Bates and Jackson, 1980).

SURFICIAL DEPOSITS

The surficial deposits are deposits that were derived from bedrock by weathering and erosion and transported by gravity, wind, or water. In the Devils Tower National Monument area are alluvium, which forms terraces and alluvial deposits along the Belle Fourche River, and talus and landslide deposits (colluvium), which have settled around the Tower and below the cliffs of Hulett Sandstone.

STREAM TERRACE DEPOSITS AND ALLUVIUM

The Belle Fourche River, which cuts across the southeast corner of the National Monument, has eroded, transported, and deposited material in its valley. The exposure of Devils Tower, which was originally surrounded and covered by sedimentary rocks, was primarily the work of the Belle Fourche River. As weathering and erosion break down the bedrock along the sides of the valley, the river transports and deposits the material in its bed and along its banks. These deposits contain rounded fragments of all the rock types that occur in the Belle Fourche River

Material deposited by running water is termed alluvium and the deposits are termed alluvial deposits.

Much of North America was covered by glaciers that reached their maximum in the west about 14,000 years ago. The area of Devils Tower was not glaciated; the glaciers were well to the north, but the climate during the period of glaciation was much colder and wetter than at present. The rivers of North America south of the glaciers were much bigger then as a result.

drainage area, including pieces from Devils Tower and Missouri Buttes. The material ranges in size from gravel to sand, silt, and clay.

There are two types of alluvial deposits in the Belle Fourche River valley: terraced deposits and recent alluvium. In the past, particularly during the last glacial periods, the Belle Fourche River contained more water and flowed at a higher level than at present. The extensive alluvial flats along the margins of the valley are terrace deposits of alluvium. These are the favorite areas for the homes of the prairie dogs (Fig. 12). The terraces are above the seasonal flood plain and therefore, well drained, and dry. The terraces are composed of unconsolidated material that is easily excavated.

Recently deposited alluvium occurs in the bed and along the banks of the Belle Fourche River. There are also recent alluvial deposits in the abandoned channels of the Belle Fourche River. The river is still cutting down its bed and transporting material. During periods of high water, it may cut across a bend and erode a new channel, abandoning its former channel. The material in the recent alluvial deposits is the same as in the terrace deposits.

FIGURE 12.

Prairie dog town east of Devils Tower. Town is on an alluvial terrace.

TALUS AND LANDSLIDES

Talus and landslide material (colluvium) covers much of the bedrock around Devils Tower. Talus has accumulated at the base of the Tower, below the cliffs of Hulett Sandstone, and there is a fossil talus deposit composed of sandstone and quartzite north of the Tower.

Talus from the Tower forms a broad apron that completely surrounds the Tower (Fig. 13). The talus extends from high on the shoulders of the Tower down to and across the sedimentary rocks. Locally, landslides of this talus have extended through valleys in the sedimentary rocks down almost to the level of the surrounding streams. Much of the talus nearest to the Tower is derived probably from the upper part of the Tower. Dutton and Schwartz (1936, p. 725) reported that the largest talus block they found measured 53 feet long and 18 feet across the end, and each hexagonal joint face measured about 10 feet wide. They estimated that this block weighed more than 1,150 tons.

FIGURE 13.

Photograph of Devils Tower showing talus apron around the base of Devils Tower
(U.S. National Park Service photograph)

Talus of different ages can be recognized around the base of the Tower. The youngest talus is that adjacent to the base of the Tower, and is continuing to accumulate (Fig. 14). While living near the base of the Tower in November 1954, during periods of frost action at nights one could hear blocks crash onto the talus. This would happen typically after a snowfall (Fig. 15). On a warm sunny day the snow would melt and the moisture would enter the joints in the Tower. After dark, the water would freeze and expand, which over time continues to force blocks from the Tower and build more talus. Halvorson (1980, p. 36, 37) recognized at least four ages of talus. The more recent talus, lichen covered, next to the base of the Tower (Fig. 15), is the youngest. A little farther from the Tower there are talus blocks intermixed with soil (Fig. 16). The older talus is mostly covered with soil with only occasional blocks showing above the soil (Fig. 17). The soil, according to Halvorson (1980, p. 37), has a thin A horizon over a C horizon. Farther from the Tower is a fourth talus covered with soil with an A horizon overlying a dense clay horizon about 30 cm thick. Halvorson (1980, p. 37) considered that these older talus deposits probably accumulated during the Pleistocene glacial epochs.

Soils are classified as having: topsoil, the A horizon or leached horizon; the B horizon or subsoil or the horizon of accumulation; and C horizon, the parent material from which the upper horizons were formed.

FIGURE 14.

Youngest talus at base of Devils Tower, west side.

FIGURE 15.

Photograph of snow on Devils Tower, southwest side.

FIGURE 16.
Talus of intermediate age, west side of Devils Tower.
(Tree in foreground 2 feet high)

FIGURE 17.

Talus next to oldest in age, west side of Devils Tower.

The cliffs of Hulett Sandstone that surrounds the Tower breaks off into rectangular blocks that form talus slopes at the base of the cliffs and, locally, large landslides down the slopes below the cliffs. These blocks of Hulett Sandstone range in size from a few inches to many feet in diameter (Fig. 18). The talus material from the Tower has at several places overlapped the cliff of Hulett Sandstone and become mixed with the material from the cliffs.

About 1,400 feet north of the Tower are two patches of what is believed to be talus, formed from sedimentary rocks that once surrounded the Tower (Fig. 19, A). The talus consists of fragments of medium-grained brownish-white sandstone and what is apparently a highly silicified gray or white fine-grained quartzite. The sandstone resembles that found in the Lakota Formation (Robinson, Mapel, and Bergendahl, 1964, p. 23), which lies about 200 feet stratigraphically above the Redwater Shale in the area west of the Monument.

The sandstone and quartzite occur in angular blocks that range from less than 1 inch to several feet in diameter (Fig. 19, B). The spaces between the blocks are filled with a yellowish or brownish-white sand. The Lakota Formation at one time surrounded the Tower and it is believed that these blocks are residual blocks that have not been removed by erosion.

The Lakota Formation, of Lower Cretaceous age, overlies the Morrison Formation. The nearest outcrops of this formation to Devils Tower is to the west, near Missouri Buttes.

FIGURE 18.

Talus blocks of Hulett Sandstone Member lying on Stockade Beaver Shale Member, Sundance Formation, south side of Devils Tower.

A. *Area of talus blocks*

B. *Blocks of quartzite*

FIGURE 19.
Talus blocks of sandstone and quartzite about 1,400 feet north of Devils Tower.

STRUCTURE

The structure of the sedimentary rocks that surround Devils Tower is relatively simple. Some slight folding occurs as the result of the intrusion of Devils Tower and related faulting and jointing. The structure of the igneous rock of Devils Tower is some banding as the result of the flow of magma that formed the Tower, minor faulting, and the conspicuous jointing of the igneous mass.

SEDIMENTARY ROCKS

The sedimentary rocks in the National Monument, and in the surrounding area, are gently folded into many small rolls, basins, and domes, which locally are cut by faults of small displacement. These small folds are superimposed on a large dome that is collapsed in the middle.

Devils Tower is near the middle of the collapsed dome. From one-half to about a mile from the Tower, the sedimentary rocks dip gently from 2° to 5° away from the Tower to form a broad dome. Within a radius of about 2,000 to 3,000 feet of the Tower, the dips change, and the rocks dip, in general, from 3° to 5° towards the Tower to form a shallow structural basin. In the basin itself and on the dome are several small folds. As an example, Spring No. 1, southwest of the Tower, is in the center of a

> *Structure means, or refers to, the attitude of the sedimentary rocks as the result of folding, faulting, and jointing of the rocks, either sedimentary or igneous. In addition, when a magma or molten rock intrudes an area, there may be flow banding or foliation.*

comparatively sharp syncline, or downfold, at the edge of the basin. Fossil Hill, northwest of the Tower, is another small structural basin. The beds along the top and on the north side of Fossil Hill dip from 12° to 52° S. Those on the south side of the hill, north of the road, apparently dip very gently northward.

Two faults were observed in the sedimentary rocks in the area of the National Monument. The faults are in the Hulett Sandstone west of the Park road and west of the Tower. The faults in the Hulett Sandstone are nearly vertical, with a displacement of less than 10 feet.

IGNEOUS ROCK

Halvorson (1980, pl. 2) noted flow structure in Devils Tower locally. The most conspicuous structure of Devils Tower are the joints, which are very significant in determining the origin of the Tower. One small fault that cut the igneous rock of the Tower was noted.

Halvorson (1980, pl. 2) shows three measurements of flow foliation in the rock of Devils Tower. One near the base in the northeast quarter of the Tower plunges 75° about S 16° E; another higher in the Tower and in the northeast quarter is horizontal with a strike of about N 70° W / S 70° E. The third foliation measured is near the base in the southwest quarter of the Tower and plunges 79° about S 85° W.

One of the most striking features of the Tower is its polygonal columns. Most of the columns are 5 sided, but some are 4 or 6 sided. The larger columns measure 6 to 9 feet in diameter at their bases and taper gradually upward to about 3 feet at the tops. The columns are bounded by well-developed smooth joints in the middle part of the Tower, but as the columns taper upward, the joints between them, rather than being smooth, may be wavy and some of the columns may unite. Numerous cross-fractures in the upper part of the Tower divide the columns into many small irregularly shaped blocks.

Dutton and Schwartz (1936), in their detailed study of the joints of Devils Tower, divided the Tower, based on the joints, into four different sections: the base, the shoulder, the main columnar portion, and the crest (Fig. 20). They noted that the base was massive and that it showed no columnar-type joints. They recognized three sets of joints: 1) peripheral joints that more or less parallel the periphery of the Tower, 2) radial joints that are approximately perpendicular to the peripheral joints, and 3) a set of near-horizontal joints (Dutton and Schwartz, 1936, p. 720-721). These joints divide the base into blocks 9 to 12 feet in maximum dimension (Fig. 21).

FIGURE 20.
West side of Devils Tower showing massive base, shoulder, main columnar section, and crest.

FIGURE 21.
Base and shoulder of Devils Tower, west side, showing irregular joints of base merging into almost horizontal joints of shoulder.

The shoulder is the transitional zone between the massive base and the main columnar portion exemplified by a zone in which the peripheral and radial joints merge into the columnar joints. The columnar joints on the shoulder are almost horizontal and curve upward to merge with the central columnar section. The diameter of the shoulder joints may be as much as 15 feet (Dutton and Schwartz, 1936, p. 723). These large columns, as they curve upward, often split into two or more smaller columns (Fig. 21). Dutton and Schwartz (1936, p. 722) suggested that:

> " — where the basal cliffs are well developed, the present configuration of the Tower may not differ greatly from the original shape of the intrusion."

In the central columnar section, the joints of the shoulder steepen and the dips go from about 30° to as much as 85°. The transition from the shoulder to the central section does not occur at the same elevation around the Tower, but there is a difference in elevation of more than 90 feet between the north side and the south side of the Tower, the north side being higher. This implies that the original shape of the intrusive mass was not symmetrical. The larger columns in diameter occur on the shoulder or just above the shoulder in the central columnar section. As the columns taper upward, they become smaller and less regular in outline and may merge into a singular irregularly shaped column of the crest section. This transitional boundary between the central columnar section and the crest section does not occur at the same elevation around the Tower. It is higher on the south side (Fig. 22).

The dip of a joint or fault is the angle measured from the horizontal.

FIGURE 22.

Crest section of Devils Tower, northwest side, showing irregularly shaped and cross-jointed column.

The crest section is about 60 to 150 feet thick. In this section the joint surfaces of the columns are irregular, or wavy, and are cut by nearly vertical to horizontal joints that divide the columns into blocks of a few feet to 15 feet or so in maximum dimension. Weathering along these joints has accentuated their appearance, but the rock below the joint surfaces is as fresh as the blocks in the central columnar section or the basal section. Figure 23 is a photograph of a talus block derived from the crest area of the Tower showing the cross joints and the weathering along the joints.

One fault was found in Devils Tower. It is on the northwest side near the base. The attitude of this fault at the point where it disappears below the talus is: strike, N. 41° W.; dip, 21° NE. The fault zone is 4 to 12 inches wide and is filled with a yellowish-green clay and sheared fragments of altered phonolite porphyry. The rock of the Tower below this fault is somewhat altered; the groundmass is a light greenish gray, and the normally shiny crystals of feldspar have a dull earthy luster.

The strike of a fault or joint is the bearing of a horizontal line on the fault or joint surface.

FIGURE 23.

A talus block derived from the crest area of Devils Tower showing cross-joints.

(Block about 20 feet long)

GEOLOGIC HISTORY

The geologic history of the Devils Tower area is part of that of the Black Hills region. The uplift of the Black Hills and the subsequent erosion have exposed the rocks, from which the geologic history of the area may be interpreted.

Most of the rocks within the area around the Black Hills are composed of sediments deposited by water. These sedimentary rocks, which overlie much older rocks (Precambrian), were deposited in a series of successive layers during time intervals from the Cambrian period to well into the Tertiary period. (Appendix A). Deposits in the ancient seas are represented by limestone, shale, and some sandstone; deposits on low lands adjacent to seas, such as flood plains and deltas, are represented by sandstone, siltstone, and some mudstone; and deposits along streams are represented by conglomerate, sandstone, and siltstone. Between the periods of deposition were intervals when the land was relatively high, and in certain areas all of the sediments of an earlier period were eroded away. Figure 24 is a generalized section of the sedimentary rocks of the western flank of the Black Hills, Wyoming.

System	Series	Age Ma	Stratigraphic Unit			Thickness (meters)	
Quaternary	Recent & Pleistocene	1.8	Alluvium and Stream Terraces (Unconformity)				
Tertiary	Oligocene	37.5	Whiteriver Formation (Unconformity)			0-46	
	Eocene	55	Wasatch Formation			75	
	Paleocene	65	Fort Union Formation	Tongue River Member		150-245	
				Lebo Shale Member		60-76	
				Tullock Member		150-300	
Cretaceous	Upper Cretaceous		Lance Formation			150-485	
			Fox Hills Sandstone	Colgate Member		15-30	.38-60
			Pierre Shale	Kara Bentonite Member		60±	245-455
				Monument Hill Bentonite Member		46-67	
				Mitten Black Shale Member		45-300	
				Gammon Ferruginous Member		0-300	
			Niobrara Formation			46-70	
			Carlile Shale	Sage Breaks Member		60-90	
				Turner Sandy Member		46-60	
				Lower Unnamed Member		12-40	
			Greenhorn Formation			20-110	
		100	Belle Fourche Shale (Probable maximum height of Devils Tower)			105-260	
	Lower Cretaceous		Mowry Shale			55-70	
			Newcastle Sandstone			0-30	
			Skull Creek Shale				
			Fall River Formation (Unconformity)			30-60	
		141	Lakota Formation			14-90	
Jurassic	Upper Jurassic		Morrison Formation (Base of Devils Tower)			0-46	
			Sundance Formation	Redwater Shale Member		9-60	
				Lak Member		12-25	
				Hulett Sandstone Member		17-27	
				Stockade Beaver Shale Member		15-27	
				Canyon Springs Sandstone Member (Unconformity)		0-12	
	Middle Jurassic	195	Gypsum Springs Formation (Unconformity)			0-38	
Triassic and Permian		230	Spearfish Formation			150-250	
Permian			Minnekahta Limestone			12±	
			Opeche Formation (Unconformity)			18-27	
Permian and Pennsylvanian		280	Minnelusa Formation (Unconformity)			198-245	
Mississippian	Lower Mississippian	435	Pahasapa Limestone			150-180	
			Englewood Limestone (Unconformity)			15-18	
Ordovician	Upper Ordovician		Whitewood Dolomite			15-18	
	Middle Ordovician		Winnipeg Formation (Unconformity)			18-22	
Cambrian and Ordovician		500 570	Deadwood Formation (Unconformity)			90-150	
			Precambrian				

FIGURE 24.

Generalized section of the sedimentary rocks of the western flanks of the Black Hills, Wyoming.

(After Robinson, Mapel and Bergendahl, 1964).

The oldest formation exposed in the National Monument, the Spearfish Formation, was deposited during Triassic time along flat lands bordering the sea. Arms of the sea locally invaded the area to leave deposits of gypsum, which are found near the base of the Spearfish Formation in areas outside the National Monument. The Gypsum Spring Formation was deposited in the sea in Middle Jurassic time following a period of uplift and erosion that occurred after the deposition of the Spearfish Formation. After the Gypsum Spring Formation was deposited, the sea retreated, and another period of erosion followed before Late Jurassic time when the sea invaded the area again and the Sundance Formation was deposited. The depth and conditions for deposition in this sea changed from time to time, as shown by the alternating beds of shale, limestone, and sandstone in the Sundance Formation.

Following the deposition of the Sundance Formation, there were several periods when the area was above sea level and when the sea covered the area. During the periods when it was above sea level, the higher land was eroded, and the sediments deposited at a lower level. When the area was covered by the sea, marine sediments, principally shales were deposited. Near the end of the Cretaceous period, the sea made its final withdrawal, and the sediments from late Cretaceous time to the present were deposited in fresh water.

The Black Hills uplift developed primarily during early Tertiary time, although it may have started in very late Cretaceous time. At this time the present general structural features of the Black Hills area were developed, and the igneous rocks, such as Devils Tower, were intruded (Jagger, 1901, p. 266). Following this, the Black Hills area was repeatedly uplifted, and erosion exposed the older sedimentary and intrusive rocks. Even today streams continue to strip more and more rock from the country, leaving only local deposits, such as alluvium and terrace deposits, along the valleys.

ORIGIN OF DEVILS TOWER

Since the first geologists viewed Devils Tower, there has been controversy as to its origin. Its spectacular appearance, and the fact that it was the first National Monument, which attracts many visitors including geologists, has brought it more attention than many igneous rocks in other parts of the Black Hills.

The earliest geologists to visit Devils Tower were Newton and Jenney (1880) who visited it in 1875 and gave a good description of the Tower and its composition. The earliest geologists to study Devils Tower and to comment on its origin were Carpenter (1888) and Russell (1896). Russell (1896, p. 25) considered the Tower to be an igneous intrusive or "plutonic plug." Jagger (1901, p. 264) considered the Missouri Buttes to be the center of a laccolith and Devils Tower as a remnant of a subordinate laccolith (Fig. 10). Darton and O'Hara (1907, p. 5-6) considered Devils Tower was a separate laccolith of larger extent than the present limits of the Tower and its talus, and that the Missouri Buttes represented one or several laccoliths. The interpretation of igneous masses resting on sedimentary rock platforms as laccoliths was a popular concept in the early twentieth century as a result of the classic study of the Henry Mountains of Utah by Gilbert (1877). Robinson (1956, 1960) rejected the idea that Devils Tower and Missouri Buttes were remnants of laccoliths. The talus derived from Devils Tower and Missouri Buttes is confined almost to the immediate area of these intrusives. There are no pieces of

A laccolith is an igneous intrusive into sedimentary rocks that spreads laterally at a stratigraphic horizon, forms a flat floor, and domes the overlying rocks.

igneous rock on the divides between Missouri Buttes and Devils Tower, or on the divides in any direction from these features. Pieces of phonolite porphyry that could have been derived from Missouri Buttes or Devils Tower are found for at least 15 miles downstream in terrace gravels along the Belle Fourche River. The percentage of pieces of phonolite porphyry in these terrace gravels, and in the modern alluvium of the Belle Fourche River, is low in comparison with the percentages of other rock types. There is no evidence to support the idea that these masses of igneous rock were appreciably larger than they are at present, or at least larger than the present area covered by their talus aprons.

Johnson (1907, p. 304), partly in response to Jagger's (1901) discussions on the columnar jointing in the Black Hills and the interpretation that Devils Tower was the remnant of a laccolith, and an implied statement in a geology text by Norton (Johnson, 1907, p. 304) that vertical columns would not be found in volcanic necks, was prompted to make a special study of the volcanic necks in the Rio Puerco Valley, New Mexico, which had eroded into the Mount Taylor volcanic plateau. Johnson (1907, p. 303), who had worked in the Albuquerque quadrangle, New Mexico, had a distant view of these volcanic necks, and was familiar with

Basalt: a dark aphanitic rock typically formed by cooling of basic lava, such as on the Hawaiian Islands.

the work of Dutton (1885, p. 172), who stated that in necks the basalt is columnar jointed. One of the stated purposes of Johnson's study was (p. 305):

> "To determine as far as possible what features may be used as critical evidence in discriminating between volcanic necks and remnants of eroded laccoliths or columnar sheets of lava."

Johnson (1907, p. 320) stated that he had never seen Devils Tower, and based his conclusions on Jagger's (1901) photographs and descriptions.

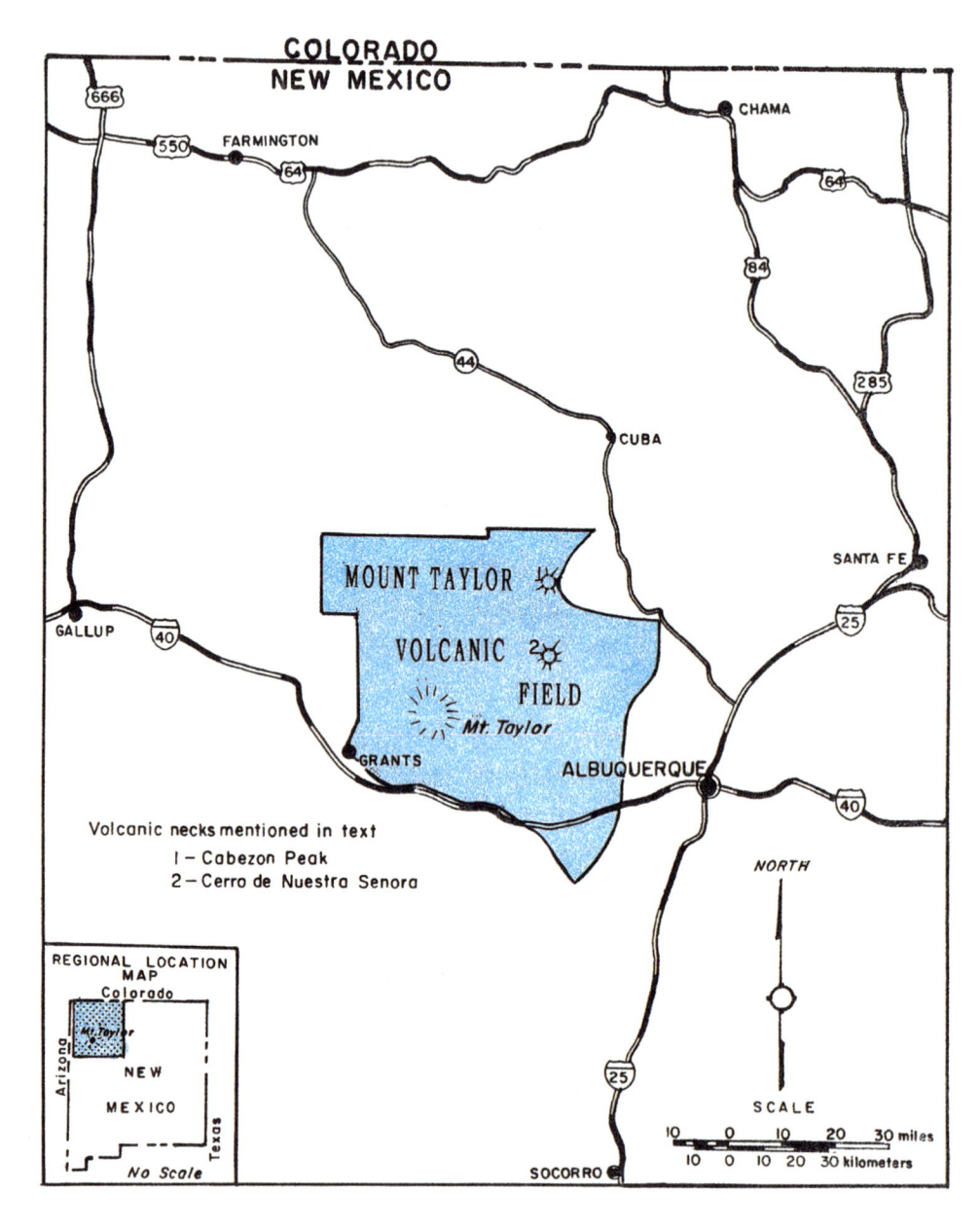

FIGURE 25.

Map showing location of Mount Taylor volcanic field, New Mexico.

Johnson's (1907) work was noted by most who worked in the Black Hills, including Darton (1909, p. 69). One of Johnson's final conclusions (p. 305) is very applicable:

> "In general, it appears that the selection of any specific structural feature as a guide to the critical distinction between volcanic necks and remnants of laccoliths or columnar sheets of lava is unsafe."

Those proponents of Devils Tower as a volcanic neck, who have referred to the work by Johnson, have ignored what, in our opinion, is very important in determining the origin of Devils Tower. That is, the composition, texture, and structure of the rock and breccia of the Mount Taylor volcanic necks as compared to that of Devils Tower and Missouri Buttes.

Hunt (1938), in his study of the igneous geology and structure of the Mount Taylor volcanic field, noted (p. 67-68) that some of the necks were composed mostly of basalt, and that some were composed mostly of breccia, but that most of them were a mixture of basalt and basaltic breccia. The breccia consists of inclusions of scoriaceous basalt that shows flow structures, and sedimentary rock derived from the intruded sandstone and shale. The breccia fragments are in a friable glassy matrix that commonly has a distinct flow structure. Typically, the breccia is cut by small dikes of basalt. One neck (Seboyeta Peak, Hunt, 1938, p. 69-70) consists of andesite and andesite breccia.

Scoriaceous: an igneous rock with many small to large holes caused by gas bubbles at the time it was lava or molten rock.

Hunt (1938), in his study, confirmed the work of Dutton (1885) that the Mount Taylor volcanic field was once an extensive plateau of hundreds of square miles that was formed by the extrusion of basalt. Much of the basalt came up through relatively small vents and spread out across an area of relatively low relief. Subsequent erosion, such as in the Rio Puerco Valley, has exposed many of the vents in which breccia and basalt have solidified and are now termed volcanic necks. It can be seen in these that there was more than one period of volcanic activity. As the vent was forced open, there was intrusion of basaltic breccia that included fragments of sedimentary rock from the adjacent intruded rocks. On breaching the surface, the breccia was intruded by basalt (Hunt, 1938, p. 30), which then flowed out across the plateau. This intrusion of basalt was not just a one-time event, but rather periods of activity followed by periods of relative quiescence, and then a renewed outflow of basalt as evidenced by superimposed flows around a vent and conspicuous flow structures within the vent, similar to what is happening in Hawaii at the present time. Cinder cones, as a result of the gas exploding in the basalt as it neared the surface, built up around the vents. With time, activity stopped and the basalt in the vent cooled and formed columnar joints. The columnar joints in many of the necks does resemble that at Devils Tower. Hunt (1938, p. 68-70) noted at Cabezon Peak and Cerro de Nuestre Se–ora, that the columns at the top were near vertical and flared out towards the base.

Figure 26 is a schematic diagram showing the origin of the volcanic necks in the Mount Taylor volcanic field. Basalt and basalt breccia were forced up through the sedimentary rock and formed vents. Basaltic lava from the vents, with repeated eruptions, spread out to form a broad basalt plateau with small cinder cones on the plateau (A). This is similar to the basalt plateau in the Snake River area of Idaho or the Columbia River basalt plateau in Washington. With time, portions of the plateau were removed by erosion leaving the columnar jointed volcanic necks (B).

FIGURE 26.

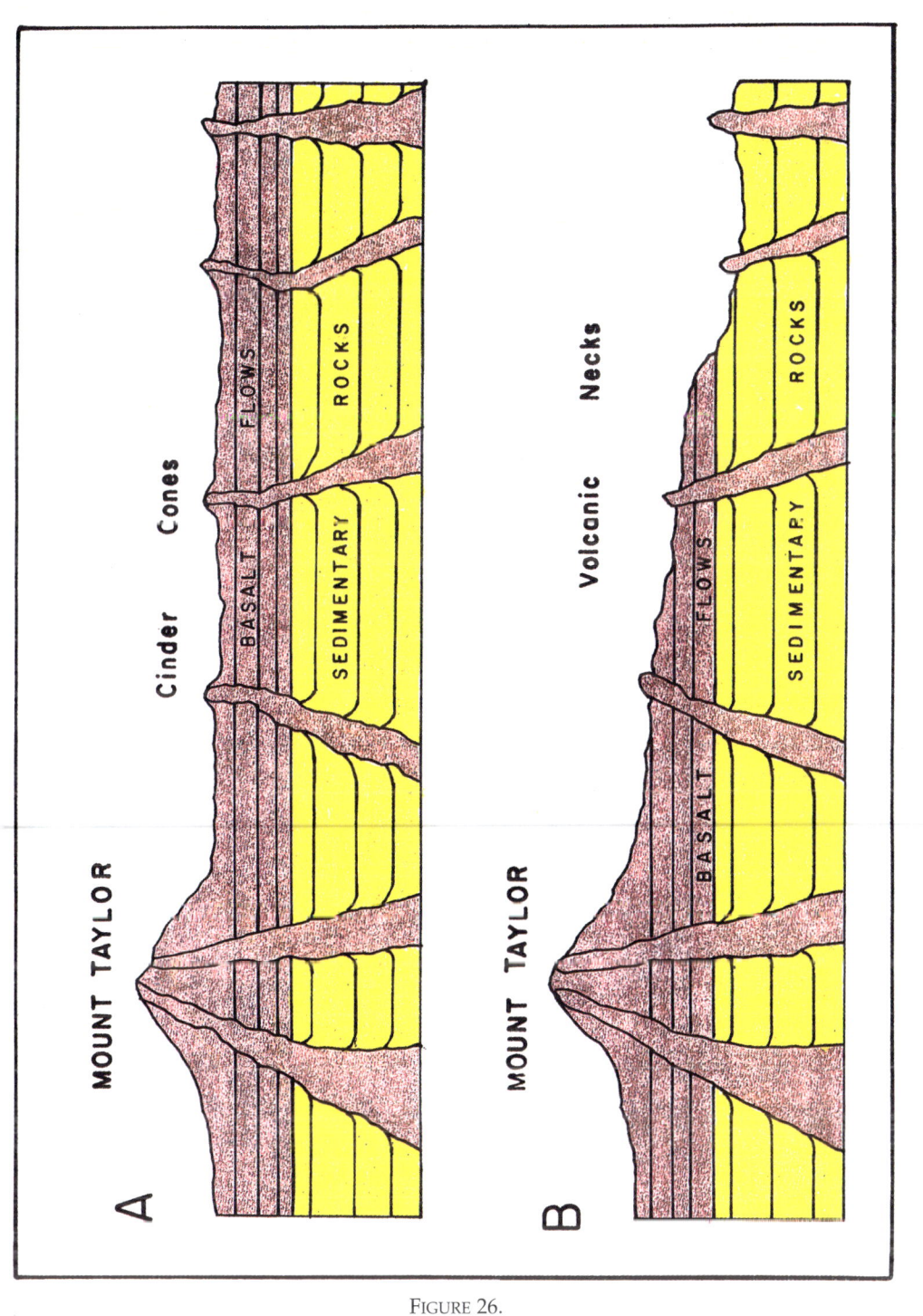

Schematic diagram showing the origin of the volcanic necks of the Mt. Taylor region, New Mexico. A, prior to erosion, B, after erosion.

Figure 27 is a photograph of Cabezon Peak, which Hunt (1938, p. 68) stated is the highest, and most impressive, of the volcanic necks. (Fig. 25). This neck has a basaltic breccia around the base of the basaltic core and highly scoriaceous basalt on top. Figure 28 illustrates the columnar jointing of Cabezon Peak, which is poorly developed as compared to Devils Tower.

Cerro de Nuestra Se–ora is another volcanic neck in the Mount Taylor volcanic field. (Fig. 25). This neck was referred to as Great Neck by Dutton (1885) and Johnson (1907), and La Se–ora Peak by Hunt (1938, p. 69). According to Hunt, most of the intrusive is basaltic breccia, but on the south is basalt. The columnar joints are near vertical, except near the base where they flare out. Figure 29 is a photograph of Cerro de Nuestra Senora, from the west, showing that it is underlain by sedimentary rock.

FIGURE 27.

Cabezon Peak, showing outcrops of sandstone at base, talus apron, and columnar joints, Mt. Taylor volcanic field, New Mexico.

FIGURE 28.

Columnar joints, Cabezon Peak, Mt. Taylor volcanic field, New Mexico.

Devils Tower, in contrast to the volcanic necks of the Mount Taylor region, is uniform in composition and grain size throughout its exposed area. This implies that there was an intrusion only at one time and not periodic activity and quiescence, which would be recognized by flow structures and variations in grain size. Halvorson (1980, pl. 2) did measure the bearing and plunge of flow lineation at three places, two of which were vertical or near vertical, and one horizontal.

FIGURE 29.
Cerro de Nuestra Se–ora, from the west, showing sedimentary rock below base. Mt. Taylor volcanic field, New Mexico.

The breccia at Devils Tower and Missouri Buttes is very different than that associated with the volcanic necks in the Mount Taylor region. Hunt (1938, p. 72) considered the breccia to be the result of progressive alteration and incorporation of roof rock by the rising intrusive. As the intrusive forced its way upward, there would be a complete gradation downward from undisturbed roof rock to scoriaceous basalt breccia containing fragments of roof rock to unadulterated basalt. At the interface of the roof rock and the intrusion there would be cooling of the basalt and incorporation of scoriaceous blocks into the breccia with pieces broken off the country rock. With continued intrusion, some of the breccia would be pushed aside to form a shell around the basalt column. Small dikes from the central basalt column cut across the bordering breccia.

The breccia at Devils Tower and Missouri Buttes consists of fragments of rocks from Precambrian igneous and metamorphic rocks and includes Paleozoic and Mesozoic sedimentary rocks. The fragments are well rounded and are incorporated in a highly altered or weathered matrix. No fragments of phonolite porphyry, or what could be interpreted as pieces of chilled border of a phonolite porphyry, have been reported. The composition of this breccia would imply that a magma under high pressure forced itself into the country rock and broke the country rock ahead of the column. The broken country rock was forced aside to form the marginal breccia. This breccia was dragged along by the magma column as it advanced upward. The upward movement was probably a slow but steady movement over a long period of time. The grain size of the phonolite porphyry would indicate that the Tower cooled at a greater depth than the exposed necks of the Mount Taylor region, which reached the surface. Hunt (1938, p. 68) stated that the scoria on Cabezon Peak is probably the remnant of the cinder cone built on the surface at the time of eruption.

The mineral composition of the phonolite porphyry of Devils Tower is considerably different from that of the basalt of the Mount Taylor region, which is indicative of the differences in the chemical composition of the magmas and their temperatures at the time of intrusion. The major minerals of Devils Tower (Table 1) are approximately sodium/potassium feldspar 49 percent, analcime 29 percent, aegine-augite 18 percent, and accessory minerals 4 percent. Hunt (1938, p. 68), reported the mineral composition of the basalt at Cabezon Peak as calcic plagioclase (feldspar) 60 percent, olivine 15 percent, augite 20 percent, and magnetite 5 percent. Phonolites are considered silicic to intermediate rocks whereas basalts are considered basic rocks.

The type of volcano that may develop is related to the characteristics of the magma. Basaltic magmas, which are lowest in silica content (± 50 percent), have the highest melting point and typically form magmas (Francis, 1976, p. 131). Rhyolitic magmas, which are highest in silica content (>65 percent), have the lowest melting point and typically form pyroclastic deposits. The phonolite porphyry of Devils Tower, with an average silica content of about 62 percent (Halvorson, 1980, Table 19), would be between the two extremes but closer in silica content to the rhyolitic magma than the basaltic magma. The Mount Taylor magmas are mostly basaltic.

The behavior of a magma depends upon the temperature, which dictates its viscosity. The viscosity dictates the explosive

Silica, SiO_2, is a common constituent of most igneous rock forming minerals.

potential of the magma and the explosiveness dictates whether the eruptive material at the surface is primarily lavas or pyroclastics (Francis, 1976, p. 132). The basaltic magmas of the Mount Taylor area flowed out as lavas and covered an extensive area of low relief, as would be expected from their composition. The magmas of Devils Tower, and those of the other igneous rocks along the western flanks of the Black Hills (Fig. 31), which are equivalent in composition to those of Devils Tower (Darton, 1909, p. 66-73), have silica contents between intermediate lavas (± 60) and rhyolitic magmas (>65 percent, Francis, 1976, p. 131). These magmas, if they reached the surface, probably would produce highly viscous lava flows, pyroclastics, or pyroclastic flows.

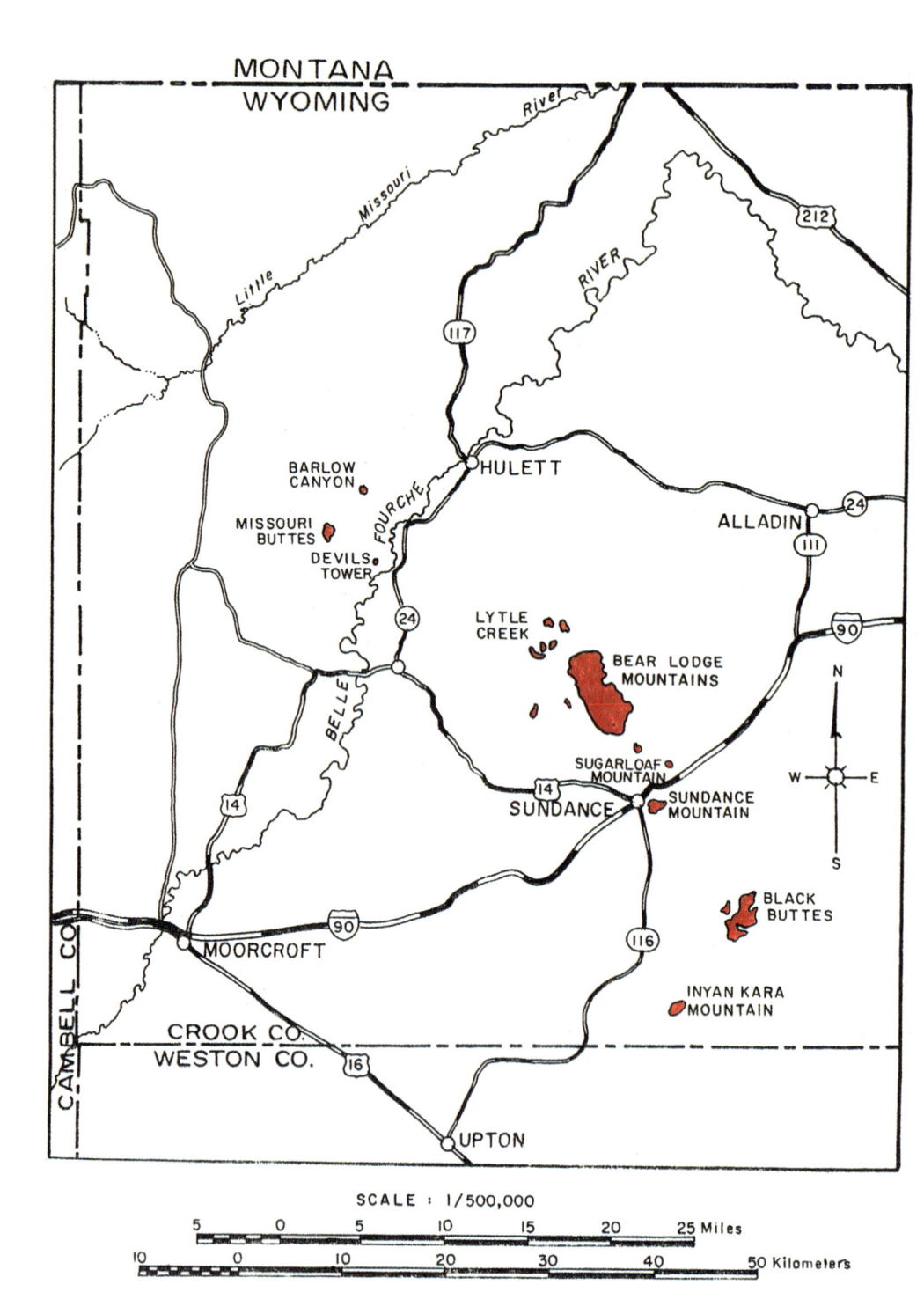

FIGURE 30.

Map showing locations of intrusive rocks, western Black Hills, Wyoming.

In mapping more than 5,000 square miles of the geology around the western flank of the Black Hills from near Newcastle, Wyoming, to beyond Alzada, Montana (Robinson, Mapel, and Bergendahl, 1964), no lavas or pyroclastic deposits were identified. Staatz (1983, p. 22) did identify two small areas of pyroclastic deposits in the southern Bear Lodge Mountains (Fig. 31). He interpreted that these pyroclastic deposits indicated that the Tertiary intrusives of the Bear Lodge Mountains breached the surface, and that these pyroclastics are preserved in Tertiary valleys. The pyroclastic deposits consist of volcanic breccia and tuff. The volcanic breccia consists of subangular to subrounded fragments of volcanic rock set in a glassy matrix. The tuff fragments are composed principally of volcanic glass, aphanitic volcanic rocks full of microlites, and porphyritic volcanic rocks. In no way do these deposits resemble the breccias found at Devils Tower and Missouri Buttes. Staatz (1983, p. 24-25) also found intrusive breccias, which contained, in addition to fragments of igneous rock, granitic fragments, probably Precambrian, and quartzite of the Deadwood Formation, (Fig. 24), similar to that found in the breccia at Devils Tower. The silica content of the phonolite of Devils Tower and Missouri Buttes is almost equivalent to that found in the pyroclastic flows of July and October 1980 from Mount St. Helens, Washington (Lipman, et al, 1981, p. 633), and cannot be compared to basaltic flow or to breccias of the Mount Taylor region of New Mexico.

Microlites: microscopic crystals.

In this zone of igneous intrusives that extends from Inyan Kara Mountain to Missouri Buttes (Fig. 31) are several folds. The folds are almost circular in plan and have steeply dipping flanks that flatten abruptly at their outer edges. Igneous rock is exposed in the domes at Missouri Buttes, Devils Tower, Barlow Canyon, Lytle Creek, Sundance Mountain, Black Buttes, and Inyan Kara Mountain. Igneous rock (phonolite), was drilled into in a dome about a mile southwest of Missouri Buttes and at Poison Creek (T. 54 N., R. 67 W., Robinson, Mapel, and Bergendahl, 1964, p 1.1). There are other domes in this belt that have not been drilled, or if drilled, did not encounter igneous rock, but as Darton (1909, p. 73) stated:

> " ... the dome structure is precisely similar to that in uplifts in which erosion has exposed the igneous core, it is difficult to ascribe them to any other cause."

In other words, the domes are the result of the intrusion of igneous plugs, equivalent to that at Devils Tower, which have not yet been exposed by erosion.

The sedimentary rocks exposed in the Black Hills area and to the west in the Powder River Basin area (Fig. 24) are nearly everywhere concordant in dip from the Deadwood Formation of Cambrian age to the Wasatch Formation of Eocene age (Robinson, Mapel and Bergendahl, 1964). Unconformities are present in the sequence and some of them represent considerable intervals of erosion, or at least of nondeposition. At most places pre-Tertiary folding was probably very gentle. The Laramide orogeny was initiated in late Cretaceous time with uplift and the retreat of the Cretaceous sea (Dickinson, et al, 1988). With continued uplift, shallow basins developed east of the overthrust belt in Idaho, Wyoming, and Utah. The Powder River Basin developed west of the Black Hills and received sediment primarily from the west and drained to the east across the area of the Black Hills (Brown, 1992). There is no evidence of uplift of the Black Hills in the Powder River Basin sediments (Seeland, 1988) through the deposition of the Wasatch of late Paleocene or early Eocene age, on the order of 55 Ma (Van Eysinga, 1975). The arc of magmatism migrated from north of the Black Hills southwest across the area of the Black Hills from 60 Ma to 40 Ma (Dickinson and Snyder, 1978). The paleogeographic studies support the age determinations on the igneous rocks for the Western Black Hills (Table 2), which were intruded in the period of 55 Ma to 38 Ma (McDowell, 1971, p. 14-15, Hill et al, 1975, p. 61; Staatz, 1983, p. 25-26). This would be within the time period from late Paleocene through the Eocene. (Appendix A). It is interesting to note that the intrusives to the west (Devils Tower, Missouri Buttes) are older, in general, than those in the Bear Lodge Mountains to the east.

Table 2 - Ages of intrusive igneous rocks, western flank Black Hills, Wyoming

Sample Location	Sample Description	Analytical Method & Minerals	Age* m.y.	Reference
Central intrusive core Bear Lodge Mountains	Phonolite and Trachyte	K/Ar Hornblende/Aegirine Augite/Hornblende	38.8 ± 2.1 48.9 ± 1.6	McDowell, 1971, p. 14
Dike U.S. Forest Service Fire Lookout Tower	Phonolite	K/Ar Sanidine	50.5 ± 0.8	Staatz, 1983, p. 25, 26
Dike NW of Tower, Warren Peak	Phonolite	K/Ar Sanidine	38.3 ± 0.6	
Central Core, North end	Trachyte	K/Ar Sanidine	50.5 ± 1.2	
West Flank, Central Core	Phonolite	K/Ar Sanidine	48.8 ± 1.7	
DEVILS TOWER					
Devils Tower	Phonolite	Fission track Sphene	53.3 ± 6.8	Hill, Izett, and Naeser, 1975, p. 61
Devils Tower	Phonolite	K/Ar alkali feldspar	40.5 ± 1.6	Bassett, 1961, p. 1373
MISSOURI BUTTES					
Missouri Buttes	Phonolite	K/Ar aegirine	49.6 ± 1.7	McDowell, 1971, p. 15
Missouri Buttes	Phonolite	Fission track Sphene	55.5 ± 7.1	Hill, Izett, and Naeser, 1975, p. 61

Range 38.3 to 55.5 m.y. 17.2 m.y.

*Ages determined from feldspars are, in general, younger than those determined on ferromagnesium minerals and ages determined by fission track on sphene are older for the same rock.

The White River Formation of Oligocene age, was deposited on an erosion surface developed on a Tertiary intrusive in the Bear Lodge Mountains (Staatz, 1983, p. 26) of approximately 50 Ma. The igneous rocks and the uplift of the Black Hills occurred between 55 Ma and 38 Ma.

How far the magma that formed Devils Tower rose through the sedimentary rock sequence is the basis for this debate. At the time of the intrusion of Devils Tower (50 ± Ma), the total stratigraphic section above the present level of the top of Devils Tower was approximately 7,000+ feet — there was only approximately 3,600+ feet of sedimentary rocks between the base of Devils Tower and the Precambrian basement (Fig. 24). The uniformity in mineral composition, grain size, and texture show that the magma that cooled to form the Tower was homogeneous. The belt of intrusive rocks along the west flank of the Black Hills of almost equivalent composition shows that there was one source of magma and that probably this source was a magma chamber at a hot-spot in the crust resulting from subduction (Dickinson and Snyder, 1978). The magma from the chamber came up along a northwest-trending zone of weakness, approximately parallel to the Black Hills monocline to the southwest (Robinson, Mapel, and Bergendahl, 1964, pl. 1) and the axis of the Black Hills uplift (Darton, 1909; Dickinson, et al, 1988, Fig. 1) to the northeast. The lack of any evidence of extrusive material along the belt in intru-

Subduction: related to Continental Drift where an oceanic plate is sliding under, or subducting, a continental plate.

sive rocks, except in the Bear Lodge Mountains, where the largest exposures of intrusive rocks are, and the occurrence of domes with igneous cores not yet exposed by erosion, would support the idea that the magma that formed Devils Tower stopped rising several thousand feet below the surface. The conclusion that Devils Tower, or the Missouri Buttes, did not vent is further supported by the absence of any lava or pyroclastic materials in the White River Formation. The White River Formation consists mostly of fluvial deposits that formed largely from locally derived materials, and had there been pyroclastic deposits from Devils Tower, or Missouri Buttes, in the area, they would be found in the White River Formation.

Joints form in igneous rock as magma cools. The volume of the igneous rock is less than that of the magma so the difference in volume is compensated for by the formation of joints. Columnar joints form at right angles to the cooling surface, that is, the thermal gradient. A crack is initiated when the thermal stress exceeds the tensile strength of the rock (Ryan and Sammis, 1978, p. 1295). There is a sudden release of strain, and a crack propagates until the material is elastic rather than brittle. As the cooling continues, the cracks continue to extend themselves. This is done in increments and can be detected by seismic methods (Ryan and Sammis, 1978, p. 1296). This incremental advance of the cracks is responsible for the grooves or striations seen on the columnar joint faces at right angles to the column. The diameter of a column is related to the rate of cooling and, therefore, to the rate of crack propagation. At the crest of Devils Tower, the diameter of the columns is smaller than that of the columns on the

Thermal gradient: direction of heat flow from hot to cold.

shoulder, which shows that the thermal gradient at the crest of the Tower was greater than at the shoulder; that is, the top was nearer the ground surface. Based on the knowledge that the joints form at right angles to the thermal gradient, then the gradient at the top of the Tower was almost vertical while at the shoulder the thermal gradient was near horizontal. Plotting a theoretical thermal gradient around the Tower shows that the intrusive that formed Devils Tower was probably tear-drop shaped with the small end down. Figure 32 is a reconstruction of the intrusive from which Devils Tower was developed. Figure 33 is a geologic section through Devils Tower at the present time.

FIGURE 31.

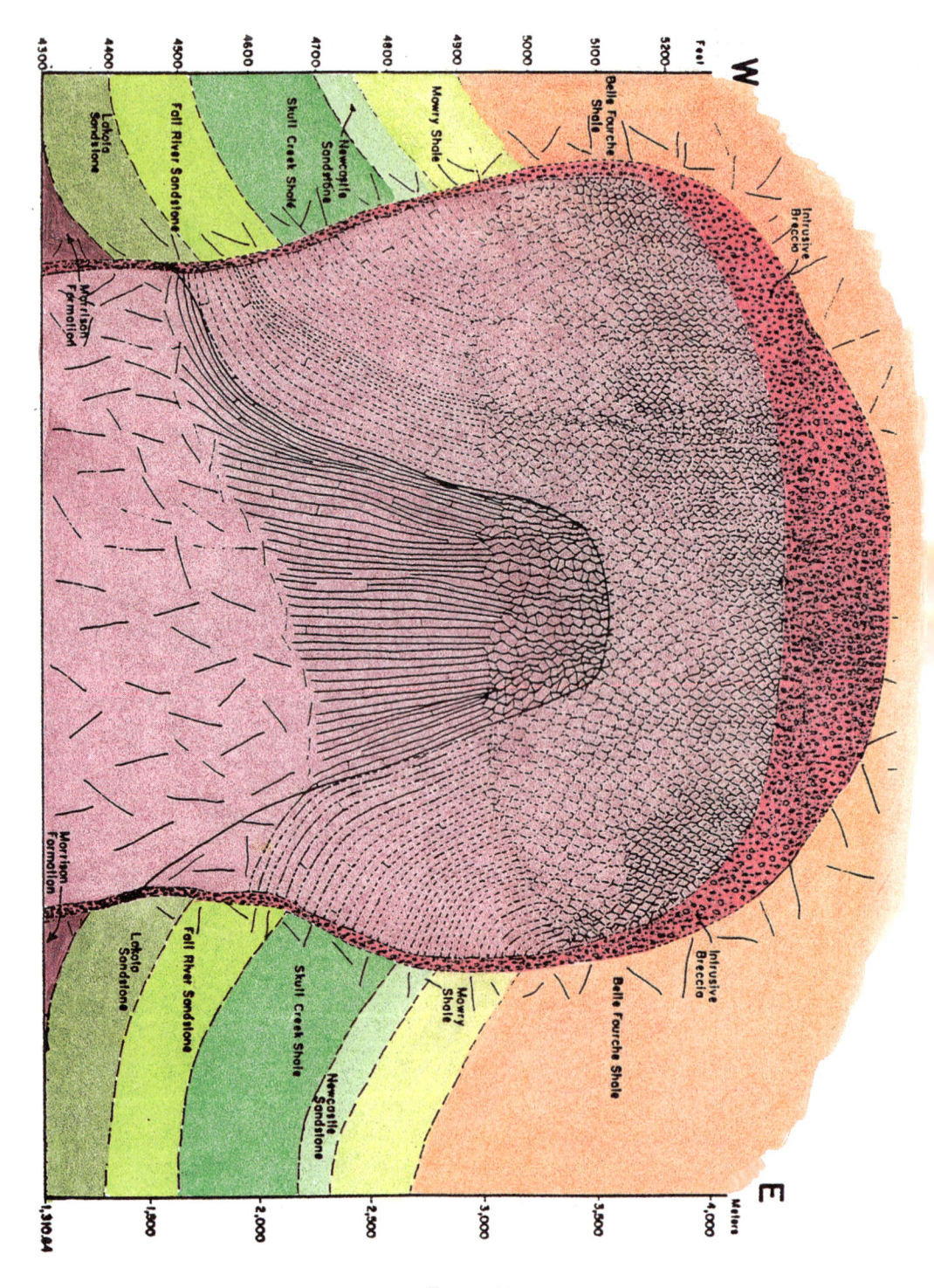

Geologic Cross-section through Devils Tower, Wyoming, at time of emplacement.

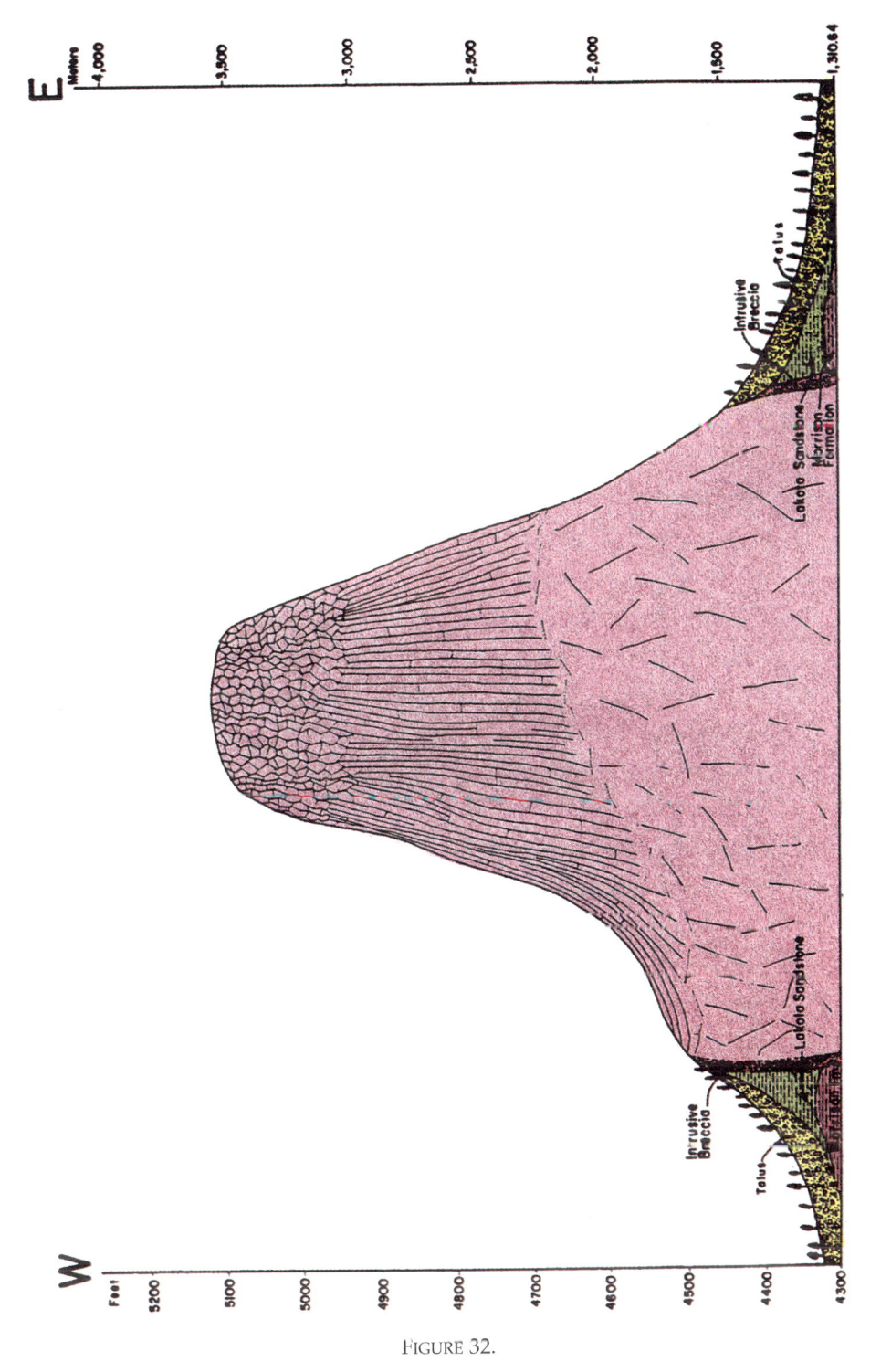

FIGURE 32.

Geologic Cross-section through Devils Tower, Wyoming, at present time.

The base of the Tower, as best as can be interpreted, rests on the Morrison or Lakota Formations. The Morrison Formation, which consists of interbedded claystones and sandstones, and Lakota Formations, which consist of interbedded sandstone below these formations are relatively well indurated siltstones, sandstones, and limestones. The overlying Fall River Formation consist predominantly of sandstone. Above these formations is a thick section of relatively soft marine shales. The initial shape of Devils Tower probably was controlled by the lithology of the enclosing rocks (Fig. 24). The magma as it intruded along a zone of weakness domed the sedimentary rocks and then broke through the sandstones of the Lakota and Fall River Formations and pushed aside relatively easily the Cretaceous shales. With continued movement upward and outward, the magma column in the sandstone formations enlarged, giving the interpreted tear-drop shape to the intrusive. The upward movement of the magma stopped when the lithostatic load on the expanded upper end of the intrusive equalled the pressure from the magma chamber minus the friction of the sides of the intrusive. After the intrusive reached its maximum extent, the pressure in the magma chamber dropped, and there was subsidence in the center of the Devils Tower dome, as evidenced by the reversal in dip of the sedimentary rocks adjacent to the Tower.

The transition zone from the shoulder of Devils Tower to the base is a critical zone in the thermal gradient. Dutton and Schwartz (1936, p. 721) identified three joint sets: N. 40-90 E., N.-N 60 W., with steep dips, and a set that dipped at 45° or less. Joint sets such as these are typical of those that develop in igneous intrusives that have cooled at depth under a low thermal gradient (Billings, 1972, p. 169) and develop as the lithostatic load is reduced by erosion.

The crest of Devils Tower is very different from the main columnar section (Fig. 22). From observations of the crest and the examination of blocks that have fallen from the crest (Figs. 15, 23), it can be seen that the columnar joint surfaces are irregular or wavy, almost like accordion pleats, and there are two distinct sets of joints: 1) at right angles to the columns, and 2) parallel to the columns but at approximately right angles to the column faces. The frequency of both the horizontal and vertical joints decreases from the top of the Tower downward and the crest zone imperceptibly grades into the central columnar section. Dutton and Schwartz (1936, p. 724) and Halvorson (1980, p. 33) attributed the difference in the appearance of the crest from that of the main columnar mass to the effects of being exposed for a longer period of time to weathering. Weathering, however, cannot account for the wavy nature of the columnar joint surfaces and the cross joints, which go completely through the columns. The crest section of the Tower is more weathered than the lower part, and this is due to the numerous cross joints that exposed more of the rock to the effects of weathering.

The characteristics of the crest section of Devils Tower can be attributed to the cooling history of the intrusive mass. The upper bulbous end of the intrusive mass supported the lithostatic load of about 7,000 feet of sedimentary rock (Fig. 24). There was a reduction of the pressure on the intrusive and a withdrawal of magma as shown by the reversal of the dips of the sedimentary rocks next to the Tower. The maximum thermal gradient was vertical and cooling was initiated at the contact of the surrounding breccia with the sedimentary rock. As cooling progressed, at a decreasing rate with depth, a crust that ranged from solid to semiplastic developed over the top of the magma column. The lithostatic load compressed the crust and semiplastic material, creating the wavy structures in the forming columns, and is probably responsible for the development of the cross and longitudinal joints within the columns. As the thickness of this section increased, it became equivalent to an arch and transferred the lithostatic load to the enclosing sedimentary rocks. For the central columnar part of the Tower, the only stress was the stress developed as the result of cooling and the columns developed by crack propagation, as described by Ryan and Sammis (1978).

SUMMARY AND CONCLUSIONS

Devils Tower is a conspicuous topographic feature on the western flank of the Black Hills of Wyoming. It is one of several phonolite porphyries that intruded the sedimentary rocks along the western flanks of the Black Hills between about 55 Ma and 38 Ma. The intrusives domed the sedimentary rocks that they intruded, but there was some withdrawal of magma and subsidence of the center of the domes after the intrusions stopped. Most of the intrusives did not vent to the surface to form volcanoes. Some pyroclastic material was noted by Staatz (1983, p. 22) in the Bear Lodge Mountains to the east, but none has been identified in the White River Formation, which is younger than Devils Tower. Some of the intrusives have not been exposed by erosion of the enclosing sedimentary rocks, and these are represented by sharp domes, some of which have been drilled and have encountered igneous rock.

The most striking feature of Devils Tower are the columnar joints. Columnar joints are also conspicuous in the other exposed igneous masses. On the basis of the joints, and the distribution of the intrusives, the origin of Devils Tower has been considered to be the remnant of an intrusive that did not reach the surface (Carpenter, 1888; Russell, 1896; Robinson, 1956), a remnant of a laccolith (Jagger, 1901; Darton and O'Hara, 1907; Effinger, 1934), and the remnant of a volcanic neck (Johnson, 1907; Dutton and Schwartz, 1936; Halvorson, 1980). The basis for considering Devils Tower a volcanic neck was the similarity of joints to that seen in the volcanic necks of the Mount Taylor volcanic field of New Mexico. It is interesting to note that Johnson (1907) never saw Devils Tower and that Dutton and Schwartz (1936), and Halvorson (1980), never visited, or at least they never reported visiting the Mount Taylor volcanic field. The volcanic necks of New Mexico consist of basalt and basalt breccia or andesite

(Hunt, 1938) and were feeders to multiple lava flows that formed the Mount Taylor volcanic field. There were eruptions from each vent, which can be determined by flow structures in the lava and breccia. Devils Tower is almost homogeneous in composition and texture. It is intermediate to silicic in composition as compared to basalt, which is basic. The joints in the volcanic necks are poorly developed as compared to that at Devils Tower, and indicate that the cooling — and jointing — occurred at a relatively shallow depth as compared to the depth of cooling for Devils Tower.

On the basis of a study of the regional and local geology at Devils Tower and the mineral composition, texture and structure of Devils Tower, it is concluded that Devils Tower represents an intrusive that penetrated the sedimentary rock to the level of the Lower Cretaceous shale about 7,000 feet below the surface. The upper part of the intrusive expanded in the relatively soft shales, then formed an inverted tear-drop-shaped intrusive. The intrusive did not extend much higher than the present height of the Tower and the diameter near its upper limit was not much greater than the diameter of the talus apron around the base of the Tower.

FIGURE 33.
Devils Tower at Sunset, west face.

ACKNOWLEDGEMENTS

At the request of the authors, this paper was critically reviewed by Dr. Harry D. Good, Professor of Geology, University of Utah (Retired) and Glen A. Izett, Research Geologist, U.S. Geological Survey (Retired). Both had worked in the western flank of the Black Hills and were familiar with the geology. Their critical reviews added significantly to the clarity and accuracy of this paper. Their time and effort is greatly appreciated. The format used was taken from that used by the U.S. Geological Survey in their publication, "Earthquakes & Volcanoes." The word processing was done by Shirley M. Schmuki of Custom Word Processing.

REFERENCES

Bassett, W.A., 1961, Potassium-argon ages of Devils Tower, Wyoming: Science, v. 134, no. 3487, p. 1373.

Bates, R.L., and Jackson, J.A., 1980, Glossary of geology: American Geological Institute.

Bergendahl, M.H., Davis, R.E., and Izett, G.A., 1961, Geology and mineral deposits of the Carlile Quadrangle, Crook County Wyoming: U.S. Geological Survey Bulletin 1082-J, p. 613-706.

Billings, M.P., 1972, Structural geology (3d ed.): Englewood Cliffs, N.J., Prentice-Hall, 606 p.

Brown, J.L., 1992, Sedimentology and depositional history of the lower Paleocene Tullock Member of the Fort Union Formation, Powder River Basin, Wyoming and Montana: U.S. Geological Survey Bulletin 1917-L, 42 p.

Carpenter, F.R., 1888, Notes on the geology of the Black Hills: South Dakota School of Mines Preliminary Report, Rapid City, S.D., 171 p.

Darton, N.H., 1909, Geology and water resources of the northern portion of the Black Hills and adjoining regions in South Dakota and Wyoming: U.S. Geological Survey Professional Paper 65, 105 p.

Darton, N.H., and O'Hara, C.C., 1907, Description of the Devils Tower quadrangle, Wyoming: U.S. Geological Survey Geological Atlas, Folio 150.

Davis, R.E., and Izett, G.A., 1962 [1963] Geology and uranium deposits of the Strawberry Hill quadrangle, Crook County, Wyoming: U.S. Geological Survey Bulletin 1127, 86 p.

Dickinson, W.R., and Snyder, W.S., 1978, Plate tectonics of the Laramide orogeny: Geological Society of America Memoir 151, p. 355-366.

Dickinson, W.R., Klute, M.A., Hayes, M.J., Janecke, S.U., Lundin, E.R., McKittrick, M. and Olivares, M.D., 1988, Paleogeographic and paleotectonic setting of Laramide sedimentary basins in the Central Rocky Mountains region: Geological Society of America Bulletin, v. 100, p. 1023-1039.

Dutton, C.E., 1885, Mount Taylor and Zuni Plateau: U.S. Geological Survey 6th Annual Report, p. 166-179.

Dutton, C.E., and Schwartz, G.M., 1936, Notes on the jointing of the Devils Tower, Wyoming: Journal of Geology, v. 44, no. 6, p. 717-728.

Effinger, W.L., 1934, A report on the geology of Devils Tower National Monument: U.S. National Park Service, Berkeley, California, 14 p.

Francis, Peter, 1976, Volcanoes: Penguin Books, 368 p.

Gilbert, G.K., 1877, Geology of the Henry Mountains: U.S. Geographical and Geological Survey of the Rocky Mountain Region, 106 p.

Halvorson, D.L., 1980, Geology and petrology of the Devils Tower, Missouri Buttes, and Barlow Canyon area, Crook County, Wyoming: Ph.D. Dissertation, University of North Dakota.

Hill, D.J., Izett, G.A., and Naeser, C.W., 1975, Early Tertiary fission track ages of sphene from Devils Tower and Missouri Buttes, Black Hills, northeastern Wyoming (abs). Geological Society of America Abstracts with Programs, Rocky Mountain section meeting, 1975, p. 613-614.

Hunt, C.B., 1938, Igneous geology and structure of the Mount Taylor volcanic field, New Mexico: U.S. Geological Survey Professional Paper 189-B, p. 51-80.

Imlay, R.W., 1947, Marine Jurassic of the Black Hills area, South Dakota and Wyoming: American Association of Petroleum Geologists Bulletin, v. 31, no. 2, p. 227-273.

Jagger, T.A., Jr., 1901, Laccoliths of the Black Hills: U.S. Geological Survey Annual Report 21, pt 3., p. 163-290.

Johnson, D.W., 1907, Volcanic necks of the Mount Taylor region, New Mexico: Geological Society of America Bulletin. v. 18, p. 303-324.

Lipman, P.W., Norton, D.R., Taggart, J.E., Jr., Brandt, E.L., Engleman, E.E., 1981, Composition variations in 1980 magmatic deposits: in Lipman, P.W., and Mullineaux, D.R. eds: The 1980 eruptions of Mount St. Helens, Washington: U.S. Geological Survey Professional Paper 1250.

Mattison, R.H., 1967, Devils Tower National Monument - its History: Devils Tower Natural History Association, 20 p.

McDowell, F.W., 1971, K-Ar ages of igneous rocks from the Western United States: Isochron/West no. 2, p. 1-20.

Newton, Henry, and Jenney, W.P., 1880, Report on the geology and resources of the Black Hills of Dakota: U.S. Geographical and Geological Survey, Rocky Mountain Region, 556 p.

Pirsson, L.V., 1894, on some phonolite rocks from the Black Hills: American Journal of Science, 3rd ser., v. 47, p. 341-344.

Robinson, C.S., 1956, Geology of Devils Tower National Monument, Wyoming: U.S. Geological Survey Bulletin 1021-I, p 289-302.

_____, Origin of Devils Tower, Wyoming [abs]: Geological Society of America Bulletin, v. 71, no. 12, pt. 2, p. 2040.

Robinson, C.S., Mapel, W.J., and Bergendahl, M.H., 1964, Stratigraphy and structure of the northern and western flanks of the Black Hills uplift, Wyoming, Montana, and South Dakota: U.S. Geological Survey Professional Paper 404, 134 p.

Russell, I.C., 1896, Igneous intrusions in the neighborhood of the Black Hills of Dakota: Journal of Geology, v. iv, no. 1, p. 23-43.

Ryan, M.P., and Sammis, C.G., 1978, Cyclic fracture mechanism in cooling basalt: Geological Society of America Bulletin, v. 89, p. 1295-1308.

Seeland, David, 1988, Laramide paleogeographic evolution of the eastern Powder River Basin, Wyoming and Montana, in Diedrich, R.P., Dyka, M.A.K., and Miller, W.R., eds., Eastern Powder River Basin - Black Hills: Wyoming Geological Association, 39th Field Conference Guidebook, p. 29-34.

Staatz, M.H., 1983, Geology and description of thorium and rare-earth deposits in the southern Bear Lodge Mountains, northeastern Wyoming: U.S. Geological Survey Professional Paper 1049-D, 52 p.

Van Eysinga, F.W.B., (compiler), 1975, Geologic time table: Elsevier Scientific Publishing Company, The Netherlands.

APPENDIX A

Chart of Geologic Time

Era	Period	Epoch	Ma
Cenozoic	Quaternary	Holocene	Last 10,000 years
	Tertiary	Pleistocene	2.5
		Pliocene	7
		Miocene	26
		Oligocene	38
		Eocene	54
		Paleocene	65
Mesozoic	Cretaceous		136
	Jurassic		190
	Triassic		225
Paleozoic	Permian		280
	Pennsylvanian		325
	Mississippian		345
	Devonian		395
	Silurian		430
	Ordovician		500
	Cambrian		570
Precambrian	Proterozoic		2600
	Archean		4000+

GLOSSARY[1]

aegirine - augite: calcium-magnesium-iron aluminum silicate of the pyroxene group.

agglomerate: a chaotic assemblage of coarse rock fragments.

albite: a mineral of the feldspar group — sodium-aluminum-silicate.

alloclastic breccia: a breccia that is formed by disruption of nonvolcanic rocks.

alluvium: material transported and deposited by running water, alluvial deposits.

analcime: hydrous-sodium-aluminum-silicate mineral.

anorthoclase: an alkali feldspar, sodium-rich aluminum silicate mineral.

aphanitic: texture of an igneous rock in which the individual grains cannot be identified by the naked eye.

argillite: compact rock derived from mudstone or shale by compaction.

basalt: a dark aphanitic rock typically formed by cooling of basaltic lava, such as in the Hawaiian Islands.

basic: rocks with a relatively low percentage of silica.

bedded: deposited in layers or beds.

biotite: a mineral of the mica group.

breccia: a rock composed of fragments of other rocks.

calcareous: limy, calcium carbonate

chert: rock composed of fragments of other rocks.

claystone: rock composed of clay.

colluvium: accumulations of weathered bedrock on top of the bedrock.

conglomerate: a sedimentary rock composed of cobbles and gravel.

dip: angle of inclination of a joint or fault measured from the horizontal.

dolomite: carbonate of calcium and magnesium $CaMg(CO_3)_2$
fault: a fracture in rock that has displacement of one side relative to the other.

feldspar: sodium, potassium, calcium aluminum silicates.

fission-track dating: a method of calculating an age of a rock in years.

flint: amorphous silica oxide.

fold: a bend in a rock.

foliation: a planar arrangement of textural or structural features in any type of rock.

geologic age: the age of a rock or geologic event as defined by the geologic time scale.
        Appendix A.

glauconite: hydrous silicate of iron and potassium, mineral of the mica group.

granite: medium- to course-grained igneous rock.

gypsum: calcium sulfate $(CaSO_4)$.

hematite: iron oxide.

igneous rocks: rocks that have formed by cooling of molten material such as lava.
isotopic age: age of a material determined by the decay of radioactive elements.

isotropic: a material that transmits light at the same speed in all directions, a glass.

joint: a fracture in a rock along which there has been no displacement.

K-AR: the ratio of potassium to argon in a rock.

laccolith: igneous intrusive into sedimentary rock that spreads laterally at a stratigraphic horizon, forming a flat floor, and domes the overlying rocks.

Laramide orogeny: the period of mountain building that resulted in the Rocky Mountains.

limestone: rock composed of calcium carbonate ($CaCO_3$).

lithic: very fine grained to glassy.

lithographic: very fine grained limestone.

Ma: millions of years before the present as 40.5 Ma = 40.5 million years old.

marine rocks: formed from material deposited in oceans.

marl: soft, earthy limestone.

metamorphic rock: a rock changed by heat and/or pressure.

microcline: a mineral of the feldspar group — potassium-aluminum silicate.

mudstone: rock composed of silt and clay.

nepheline, sodium-potassium silicate mineral.

nosean: sodium-aluminum-silicate-sulfate mineral.

orthoclase: a mineral of the feldspar group — a potassium-aluminum-silicate.

ostracodes: microscopic shelled animals.

overthrust belt: a zone where older rocks are thrust over younger rocks.

paleogeographic: studies of past mountains and oceans.

pegmatite: very coarse grained intrusive igneous rock.

petrography: the study of the mineral content of rocks and the relationship of minerals.

phonocyst: a mineral grain larger than grains of ground mass.

phonolite: igneous rock primarily composed of alkali feldspar, feldspar composed of sodium or potassium silicates. Named from fact the rock rings when struck with hammer.

plutonic: of igneous origin.

porphyry: rock with conspicuously large mineral grains (phenocrysts) in an equal-granular finer grained groundmass. Rock said to be porphyritic.

pyroxene: a group of dark rock-forming minerals.

quartzite: silicified sandstone.

rhyolite: a fine-grained siliceous igneous rock

ripple marks: waves of sand found on beaches, under shallow water in oceans and lakes, and formed by currents in streams.

sandstone: rock composed of sand grains.

sanidine: a mineral of the feldspar group — potassium-aluminum-silicate.

schist: metamorphic rock, one changed by heat and pressure, that breaks into thin flat pieces.
scoriaceous: an igneous rock with many small to large holes caused by gas bubbles at the time it was lava.

sedimentary rocks: rocks composed of granular material or chemical precipitates that have been deposited by wind or water on land or in the water.

shale: rock composed of clay that breaks into thin pieces.

silicic: rocks with a high percentage of silica (SiO_2)

siltstone: rock composed of grains of silt.

silty: contains silt.

soils: classified as having topsoil, the A horizon or leached horizon; the B horizon or subsoil or horizon of accumulation; and C horizon, the parental material from which the upper horizons were formed.

sphene: calcium-titanium-silicate mineral.

stratigraphy, the science of rock strata, concerned with sequence, age, composition, fossil content, and distribution of sedimentary rock.

strike: the bearing of a horizontal line on a joint or fault surface.

subduction: related to Continental Drift where an oceanic plate is sliding under, or subducting, a continental plate.

sublithographic: lithographic limestone is a very fine grained limestone once used for preparing printing stones, i.e., lithographies. Sublithographic, not as fine grained as lithographic.

talus: blocks of bedrock at the base of a cliff (type of colluvium).

thermal gradient: direction of heat flow.

trachyte: a group of fine-grained, generally porphyritic extrusive igneous rocks.

vertebrates: animals with internal skeletons.

vesicular: small holes in an igneous rock formed by bubbles of gas at the time of its intrusion/extrusion.

zeolite: hydrous-aluminum silicate mineral, analogous in composition to feldspars.

[1] Descriptions based on Bates and Jackson, 1980, Glossary of geology: American Geological Institute.